We Survive To THRIVE!

Volume 2

We Survive To THRIVE! Volume 2
Life changing stories of breast cancer survivors to inspire and encourage all

Copyright © 2015 Paula Smith Broadnax

ISBN-13: 978-0692518472

ISBN-10: 0692518479

Cover Photo designed by ILGeorgiev

Editor: Louise McKinney, WordWorks

T. Vizion Broadnax
UNI Publish Media – UNI SUCCESS SOLUTIONS, INC
Atlanta, Georgia
uni-likesolutions.com/publish

Printed in the United States of America

Other books by **Paula Smith Broadnax**

Dreams, Hopes and Possibilities

We Survive To THRIVE! Volume 1

We Survive To THRIVE!

Life changing stories of breast cancer
survivors to inspire and encourage all

Volume 2

Paula Smith Broadnax

UNI Publish Media —
UNI Success Solutions, Inc
Atlanta, Georgia

CONTENTS

CONTENTS

ACKNOWLEDGMENTS

To the brave Authors who were willing to bear their souls by revisiting painful times in their lives so that others may hopefully benefit. I am so grateful that our paths have crossed and count it a joy to have you in my life. It is my prayer that you will continue to allow the Lord to use you to be a blessing to others.

Vizion Broadnax, UNI Publish Media – UNI Success Solutions, Inc, my exceptionally talented daughter for her vision, love and support as she thrives to support me in leaving a godly legacy for the world!

Louise McKinney, WordWorks, for sharing her editing skills on this project; but, more importantly, for seeing the vision, joining the mission and offering her unlimited support in ensuring others can share their inspiring stories with the world.

Sarah Grant, a "breast" friend, and an untiring breast cancer advocate. I am grateful for her passion and desire for this book to be diverse and full of as many God stories as possible.

Seong Kwak for sharing her expertise and knowledge; thereby, allowing us to publish a highly professional product.

Last, but by no means least…my beloved husband, Tommie, for his love and support in ALL things!

INTRODUCTION

As I journey on, I continue to meet phenomenal women (and, sometimes, men) who, like me, have survived a breast cancer diagnosis. In talking with them, I am so encouraged by the grace and strength they display after their experiences. These encounters always remind me of some common threads between each of us. Such as:

> ➤ Through a tough time in our lives, we do not regret the challenge.
> ➤ We are who we are today as a result of the experience.
> ➤ God's grace and mercy brought us through the trial.
> ➤ God has kept us here to be a blessing to others.

My desire is to create a platform for as many of them as possible to continue to share information about breast cancer awareness. My hope is that, through the publishing of their stories and leaving a written legacy for the world, our mission will be accomplished.

As with Volume 1 of *We Survive To THRIVE!* Volume 2 is sure to enlighten readers to the difference between surviving (existing) in life and thriving (flourishing, prospering and succeeding) in life. If you are inspired by these stories, remember that we are blessed to be a blessing....so share the book with someone you believe will benefit from reading it.

Peace, love and blessings…

Paula

SCRIPTURES

Jeremiah 29:11

11 For I know the thoughts that I think toward you, saith the Lord, thoughts of peace, and not of evil, to give you an expected end.

Matthew 21:22

22 And all things, whatsoever ye shall ask in prayer, believing, ye shall receive.

Proverbs 3:5-6

5 Trust in the LORD with all thine heart; and lean not unto thine own understanding.

6 In all thy ways acknowledge him, and he shall direct thy paths.

All Bible quotes are from the King James Version

FOREWORD

by

Minister Annie M. Beasley

The book, *WE SURVIVE TO THRIVE,* was originally written to encourage breast cancer survivors, and rightly so, because the authors are survivors of that dreaded disease. I am not a survivor of breast cancer; but I have survived through many dark areas of life.

The authors and their testimonies of strength have encouraged me beyond measure. You will find knowledge of how to support someone who is fighting this battle of cancer, as well as strength for yourself if family or friends may face the same fight. The book can be a gift to lift their spirit when you have no words to say. When you are going through a trial and someone else has been there, their testimony can lift you up.

The aim of *WE SURVIVE TO THRIVE* is to encourage those who or going through this battle with knowledge to *THRIVE,* no matter where they find themselves. Half the battle is our mental capacity to move forward, fight a good fight, and live a good life.

In this book you will find that we all face diversions in our lives that can, and sometimes will, stop us in our tracks, if we allow it. Within these pages, you will not find victims, but victors. The book allows us to look at the sentence and stop the wheels from turning; and to reinvent the wheels, and roll on to opportunity and a full life.

Witnesses give a direction that only a spiritual journey will take you. These are stories of women who were given a death sentence and yet live a good life much longer than doctors predicted. They have proven that God has the last word! And, by example, they encourage others to do the same.

WE SURVIVE TO THRIVE will help anyone, who desires to be strengthened, to face life challenges. Not only does it help to connect your spiritual being, it equips you with coping skills to overcome life challenges. In life, the norm is when you find yourself in a test to seek the tools to survive. In this book, the authors have provided you with proven tools prior to your test – preventive maintenance, some may call it.

These stories will not be obliterated, because it's a journey in life that we all go through. We are either in a storm, been through a storm, or coming out of a storm. No matter where you are, or find yourself, the stories in *WE SURVIVE TO THRIVE* will help you through your journey. You'll be reminded, whenever you're going through a test, to depend on God and know there are many witnesses who have been there.

Don't pick up *WE SURVIVE TO THRIVE* and skim through it! Sit down and read as a gift from the Creator and friends to remind you that He will never leave you alone.

You are an overcomer -- the battle has been fought -- and the victory is yours! Be blessed!

Minister Annie M. Beasley

Susan
Bossert

Georgia
20 -Year
Survivor/Thriver

ABOUT THE AUTHOR

Susan is in her 50's, has lived in the South for nearly 25 years and loves gardening year 'round. She is so proud of her children, Haley and Thom, who are in the midst of launching careers and completing college.

Over a 30-year career, Susan worked for top U.S. banks, such as Citibank and JP Morgan Chase, in positions of increased responsibility, rising to Senior Vice President at SunTrust.

Susan is confident, optimistic, and resilient and looks forward to the next half of her life, and all the joy God has planned for her.

With thanks to God, love for her children, gratitude for her family and her friends, and her Pastor who encouraged her, this chapter is dedicated to the memory of her late husband and sister. May their lives continue to bless others.

CHAPTER ONE

DON'T BE AFRAID, FOR I AM WITH YOU

by Susan Bossert

Cancer entered my life when I felt a lump in my breast while showering. Alone, on a business trip, I felt frightened and wondered, "Could I possibly have breast cancer?"

It was a pivotal time in my life. My husband, Peter, had been diagnosed with chronic progressive Multiple Sclerosis (MS), and he battled valiantly, but after a five-year struggle his mobility was so impaired he was forced to use a wheelchair and it was impossible for him to continue in his career in New York City. We moved south, to take advantage of the slower pace of life, and lower cost of living. We pared down to my salary and I began a new job.

Our children, Tommy and Haley, were only five years old and two years old, at the time which made the transition easy as they quickly formed friendships. This led to our meeting other young families, and soon we had developed ties in the community. Peter reinvented himself. Once a star athlete and businessman, he dedicated himself to our children and made a strong case for *"Best Father Ever."*

I was under stress as I balanced the demands of my new job with my roles of wife and mother. I tried to be Super Woman. I worked a 60- to 65-hour week, yet still was involved in my children's lives and my community. My dedication to the job paid off. I was promoted within six months; but this new role meant I had to travel frequently. I questioned if it was worth the sacrifice as I sat on my hotel bed 1,000 miles away from my family, panic-stricken and wondering if I had breast cancer. How would my family get by if something happened to me? How could our family face another trial so soon? Frantically, I called my husband and told him about the lump.

Since Peter's MS diagnosis, whenever I felt overwhelmed and alone, I clung to verses from Isaiah. I meditated on it now until my anxiety disappeared and I was able to get to work:

Do not be afraid, for I am with you.
Do not be discouraged, for I am your God.
I will strengthen you and help you.
I will hold you up with my victorious right hand.
Isaiah 41:10 (KJV)

Once home, I scheduled my first mammogram, and the results confirmed that there was a mass. A nurse scheduled an appointment with a general surgeon. I was only 34 years old at the time and I was scared.

The surgeon hung my films from a light board, and pointed to some cloudy areas which he explained looked like micro calcifications that could be cancer. He recommended a modified radical mastectomy and said I would lose my breast, some of the muscle in my chest wall, and my lymph nodes, too. Even so, he told us there was still a 50-50 chance it was not cancer! He called his nurse in to schedule this major operation. I was horrified to think part of my body, so closely tied to my femininity, would be chopped off!

Peter turned to me and asked if I knew how raccoons are tested for rabies? No, I didn't!! And, what did it have to do with this? He explained a raccoon could be caged and observed for two weeks; or, they would just euthanize the poor animal, then immediately remove its brain to examine it on the spot. If it turned out the raccoon didn't have rabies, oh well…it's still dead.

"That doctor seems pretty quick for you to walk around with one breast," Peter said. "I know you wouldn't like that. And he's not even sure you have cancer." He then explained he did some research and learned about an alternate to mastectomy that I was unfamiliar with— lumpectomy. Coincidentally, our children's pediatrician was married to a surgeon who performed the procedure.

How wise! While I went to work and worried, he researched and sought counsel. We told his nurse we wanted a second opinion, an option

I didn't even understand was available to me, and quickly left that surgeon's office.

Because of the relationship, we got an immediate appointment. The specialist took a different approach. Instead of disfiguring surgery, she planned to determine if I actually had cancer before any major cutting. She laughed at Peter's story about the raccoon and promised to get me out alive. The new surgeon instilled confidence that a mastectomy was premature, and so we scheduled the lumpectomy right before Thanksgiving. I silently prayed I would stay healthy for my family.

Surgery day started with another mammogram where a needle was inserted as a guide to locate the tumor during surgery. I was scared and silently prayed the Isaiah verses again. The anesthesiologist put me in a twilight sleep for the operation. It was a day surgery, and I was sent home that same night with narcotic painkillers.

Thanksgiving was always at my house, and although I communicated it was not a good time to visit, my parents, sister, and her family all flew in. They had no comprehension how my breast surgery kept me from roasting a turkey. That's the problem when you pretend to be Super Woman—people think you really are! To get everyone out of the house so I could rest, Peter arranged Thanksgiving luncheon at a hotel while I stayed in bed.

I was alone when I got the call. The biopsy determined I had noninvasive breast cancer called lobular carcinoma in situ (LCIS). Had I waited to act, it would have spread. Because the tumor was removed quickly, there was no additional surgery required. Chemotherapy and radiation were never even mentioned. The surgeon explained I was likely to develop cancer in the future. To lower the risk, she recommended a hormone medication. I grabbed onto "no additional surgery required" vs. "carcinoma in situ" and was relieved and grateful. When everyone returned to the house, I shared my good news. We were already dealing with MS on a day to day basis; we didn't need another illness like cancer taking over our lives, too.

By Saturday I could shower. Initially, I was willing to do anything, but now that I was okay, I was vain, mourned my breast, and afraid to face the wound. My arm was too sore, so my sister peeled off the bandage. "It doesn't look *that* bad," she said. Because I was distressed, I think that I made her upset too. She tried to fix the situation, which unfortunately came out as criticism of my marriage. To her it was ridiculous Peter gave up a lucrative career. She had no understanding or empathy of his MS. She felt she had the better situation because she stayed home with her children. She warned if I continued to care for Peter, while I raised my children and worked full time, the breast cancer would come back. She advised me to divorce; and to find someone who would support me before my looks were gone.

Our values and expectations of marriage clashed. To her, marriage was a contract; no paycheck was a deal breaker. In my eyes, Peter's worth and importance to me and to our children could not be measured in monetary terms. I believed in the sanctity of marriage, and did not see how divorce was a response to illness. Peter and I felt joined not only through the legality of marriage, but by our spiritual vow to care for, and love one another through sickness and health. No matter what challenges or blessings came our way, we were dedicated to face it together.

Once I began to read the Bible, I came to recognize the Christ-like aspects of Peter's character, such as his integrity, goodness, kindness, compassion, patience, and wisdom, which made him a wonderful example for our children to model themselves after. The amazing man that Peter was (despite the limitations and pain of his illness), and the way he joyfully dedicated himself to our family, deserved my respect and dedication. When did God promise it would be easy? I was married to the love of my life, and we had two beautiful children, and a wonderful lifestyle. Peter was our rock and the leader of our family—MS or not. I was sorry my sister could not see that.

My fear breast cancer would return, worry over Peter's unstable health, and challenges associated with having a growing family led me to question and fear God. I sought understanding and brought myself closer to His Word. It helped me to be less anxious, but I never completely surrendered. The daily struggles of Peter's MS affected my family so much that I had to put my own health concerns on the back burner. With no support from extended family, I felt as if everything fell on my shoulders and I could not slow down. I was very much a "Type A" personality.

New career opportunities arose, and I accepted them. This led us to live in three different states. Because I was high risk, I found a breast specialist each time we moved. I took the prescription to ward off a recurrence, but I was unaware of preventive surgery some women in my situation had. I just assumed eventually all of this would catch up with me, and one day I would hear, "Bingo, breast cancer is back!"

At that time five years was considered a benchmark and, if achieved, you were golden and untouchable. Once I passed the marker, I relaxed and put breast cancer out of my mind almost entirely. My relief was short lived. The very next year I found a lump and after the follow- up, surgery was recommended. As silly as this sounds, my reaction was annoyance. I did not have time for cancer!

When I tearfully called my sister, she bluntly reminded me I did not heed her warning. I was on my own! Later, when she reached out to Peter, she told him to leave me, due to her misconception that he was the cause of my poor health. Her cruel accusations were too large of a grievance for me to forgive, and we did not speak for several years. I was even more hurt when my parents sided with her.

I have found that family and friends often respond to illness in ways that we just do not anticipate. Bad news can bring out the best or the worst in someone, and looking for someone to blame is textbook. It saddened me that this was my family's response when I needed support most. I counted on family, and they failed me, and it hurt. The only place I could look for comfort and support was up. My anxiety was calmed from my belief that God is faithful and no matter what trial I may face; He will never leave me!

> *"Do not be afraid, for I am with you.*
> *Do not be discouraged, for I am your God."*
> *Isaiah 41:10*

The lumpectomy was scheduled at an outpatient breast care facility. Imagine a whole facility just for women with breast cancer. There truly was an epidemic! I thought this lumpectomy would be performed just like the earlier operation, but it was actually more high tech. It was not just one needle, but a whole handful that was inserted into my breast at multiple angles to target the mass. Once that was accomplished, I clasped my surgical gown to protect the little modesty I had left and was escorted to the operating room.

There was a vertical operating table. I was told to grab the handles, and position my breasts through the operating table holes, which was difficult considering the bouquet of needles jutting out of me. The nurse said to get comfortable (How was that possible?) as she clamped straps around me. I am claustrophobic, started to panic, and made her stop.

A nurse-anesthesiologist cranked up my medications. Once the sedative kicked in, we tried again. Now, awake but not really caring what happened, I just barely held on while the table pivoted. I went from a standing position to a flank position. The surgeon rotated the table, and raised me as if I were a car on a lift in a garage. She explained gravity and the wires would guide her to exactly where to operate so minimal tissues would be taken. It is incredible that biotech engineers could come up with this! The procedure was done under local anesthetic, and I chatted with the surgeon through the whole thing.

A few days later Peter was called and asked to bring me in for the diagnosis. That scared me! Almost the entire time I raised my children I accepted my fate as a repeat contestant in the breast cancer lottery—but actually to be selected? If the surgeon called my husband to bring me in, I must have breast cancer. I went outside to weed the flowerbeds so Peter wouldn't see me cry. I often conversed with God in the garden. I prayed for more time to care for my family.

The surgeon solemnly gave us the diagnosis—lobular carcinoma in situ. We were relieved it was another noninvasive breast cancer diagnosis like before. While the surgeon considered it serious, Peter quipped, "Been there, and done that, got the T-shirt." We laughed and smiled from ear to ear. Since there was no further action required, we had every reason to be happy.

Over a period of nearly 20 years I underwent seven surgical lumpectomies or core needle biopsies. Each time another lump was discovered, I immediately visited my doctor. I knew it was critical to my family's security that I not delay. The earlier cancer is found, the better the outcome. I put my trust in God and my surgeons to keep me here to care for my family.

The repeat breast cancer diagnosis ranged from lobular carcinoma in situ, to an accumulation of abnormal cells that needed to be monitored, to Cancer Stage 0. To hear noninvasive breast cancer repeatedly, or better yet - benign, was a blessing. While there seemed to be no rhyme or reason to the findings, there was one thing for sure—cancer was always found in the nick of time! No chemo or radiation was ever required of me. Early detection allowed my cancer to be "cured" by surgery. I was blessed to be able to continue to serve my family.

Being faced with breast cancer over and over was frightening, but I did my best to hide my anxiety from my children as their father's MS was upsetting enough. I was also careful, and never told anyone at work for fear I would be passed over for promotion, lose my bonus, or be fired and not be able to support my family.

Through the years Peter's health seriously deteriorated, and he suffered heart attacks and a stroke. Simultaneously, I had other health issues and underwent a series of operations. These other problems started to take center stage, so I missed several years of breast surveillance. How could I possibly complain? Unlike my husband's MS, each of my problems had a start, and a finish, and I could walk.

As Haley entered her freshman year of college, Peter and I were hospitalized at the same time. This was nearly overwhelming for my 18-year-old to manage. Thankfully, friends and neighbors came to the rescue. My sister broke her boycott and visited a few days to support Haley. I appreciated this, but at the same time it was a tense visit due to our damaged relationship over her false idea that my caretaking caused my illness.

While I recovered, my husband made his end of life decisions. As I anticipated the tremendous loss, God sent me a clear message. My only concerns needed to be of faith and my family. I nursed Peter; and with the love of compassionate friends and our minister, we attended to Peter's spiritual wellbeing and helped my children cope. The morning Peter died, angels came for him. While I was nearly overwhelmed with grief and sadness, there was great joy, too. Angels most definitely came for him! What more did I need to know? God is merciful and Heaven is real.

After the loss, and the epiphany Heaven is real, I wondered why I worked so hard and was so dedicated to my job versus putting my family first? It took some time to process my loss. Haley and I took several trips to bond and care for each other. My sister and I reconnected, and also took a trip. I threw myself into causes and took on projects to help others.

At the end of what I thought would be a healing year, I suddenly landed back in the hospital with a life-threatening intestinal blockage. My sister was surprised medical crises continued to plague me, even after my husband's death. Haley balanced her studies and came home from college to help. More medical drama made my son very anxious, and he took time off from the university. I love my children and I am so sorry for how my health negatively affected them. I am grateful and thankful for our two amazing children. It is their love and support, and simply God's grace that pulled me through. I recovered beautifully and knew God brought me to this day for His purpose.

The next year my sister confided she had some odd symptoms and pain. I encouraged her to see a gastroenterologist who sent her for an MRI. The diagnosis was aggressive ovarian cancer that had already spread to her intestines. Her doctor told her without immediate surgery she would die. I was stunned. My sister had barely been sick a day in her life.

"I don't deserve this! I live a healthy lifestyle. I don't have any vices. I don't deserve to be sick. I'm pissed!" She said to me over the phone.

I listened to the anger in her voice. Who does deserve cancer or any debilitating disease? She expected me to turn my back on her and say it was karma. I would never have done that. If I forgave her, comforted and served her, and showed empathy in excess of what she actually expected, might she see the Holy Spirit working in me and be touched too? Going through so many personal health challenges certainly changed me. I came to see God glorified by the compassion shown to the suffering and the sick. My sister had cancer, was angry at the injustice, and was afraid she would die. I believed in Heaven and wanted it for my sister. I could not imagine facing death without faith.

I flew up to be with her while she was hospitalized and ultimately stayed for six weeks. Her surgery was aggressive: a full hysterectomy, an appendectomy, removal of portions of the large and small intestines, 40 lymph nodes, and debulking. The disease was found in a late stage. I encouraged her to be optimistic and resilient. Thoughtfully, she admitted she admired those qualities in my late husband, Peter and that he set a high bar. Cancer and recovery from surgery made her vulnerable. Her eyes were opened. She asked forgiveness for her judgment that I caused my own illness. People say it all the time: life is too short. Her diagnosis made us realize pride kept us from forgiveness.

After almost two weeks in the hospital, I helped her transition home. There was a colostomy bag to get used to, and infections that needed attention. I cooked, did laundry, and cared for her whole household. But, because of our earlier estrangement, I was virtually unknown to her younger children. Since I personally knew the difficulty of being a caregiver, and how to navigate the medical system, I tried to support her husband and children just as much as I supported my sister. I went on a little shopping spree and gifted her with pretty nightgowns and cheerful, loose- fitting tops that hid the bag so she would still feel feminine and not be discouraged.

No sooner did I return home than a bad reaction to chemotherapy landed her back in the hospital. I flew back up and supported and cared for her and her family all over again. This went on for months. I traveled back and forth frequently, stayed for long periods of time. We made a fun afternoon of trying on wigs of all colors and lengths, and she bought several. The stylist trimmed them while my sister wore them just like she would a regular haircut so they were fashioned to be most flattering. We found the joy in the situation. Finally, she was finished with chemo and was in remission.

Once home, I started to rebuild my own life and that included dating. Before he passed Peter encouraged me to remarry after he died and because we had a happy union despite our circumstances, I believed I could find happiness again. Now, in addition to helping others, I was going out to dinner, to parties, the theatre, and even rode on the back of a Harley Davidson! After so much caretaking I wanted to surround myself with positive people, embrace life, and enjoy every minute.

My sister knew her cancer would return and she searched the Internet for treatments that might help. In her research, she realized there could be a genetic component to her cancer.

"Are you sitting down?" she said when I answered the phone. She told me she had "BRCA 1," a gene mutation officially known as "Breast Cancer 1, early onset," and that clusters were found in families of our heritage. She assumed I had it, too.

I asked her to slow down. She was the Biology major; not me. I barely caught something she said about protein, and damaged DNA...cells that grow and divide uncontrollably...I was having trouble keeping up! Weren't mutations what the X Men have? "Bottom line, there's an 87-percent risk you'll get breast cancer again. You're a ticking time bomb!"

The actress Angelina Jolie has been vocal in the press about her own family history of cancer, mutations, and preventive surgery. This was before her announcements. I had never heard of BRCA, and it just wasn't sinking in. How could we have this thing if our mother was fine?

"After I saw the genetic counselor, I asked Mom to be tested and she's negative. It had to come from Dad's side. I asked him to get tested, too. He doesn't know anything about anyone left behind in Europe, but he had cousins here with cancer. Because of BRCA, my cancer is more aggressive and will kill me in about three years." My sister said all in a matter of fact tone.

My sister could be cynical, so I tried to be encouraging and told her, "Aren't you in remission? Some women have beat ovarian cancer for 10 years. You're an over-achiever! You can do it!"

"Not me. I put the brakes on it, but I'll never be cured," she said. "This is my death sentence, but it doesn't have to be yours. The geneticist said women with BRCA get prophylactic hysterectomies and mastectomies. You had a hysterectomy already, now its time to give up your boobs."

This conversation was getting crazy! How could I have surgery if I didn't have cancer? But she was relentless. She even sent me her genetics report via FedEx. She became a fierce champion of BRCA testing. She was never bitter that she was unaware of the risk until after her diagnosis. She influenced testing for the family and people in her community; and if positive, she encouraged prophylactic surgery to prevent cancer. She was a cancer warrior!

When I met with the genetic counselor, there was barely anything to it. Usually, there's a long intake form to complete of the medical histories of close relatives, but my sister compiled all of that. All I had to do was spit into a vial to capture a DNA sample. A few weeks later it was confirmed I was positive. Since I dealt with breast tumors for nearly 20 years, this really came as no surprise to me.

I went right to see my breast surgeon. The BRCA test and my sister's cancer were game changers, and I was scheduled for an MRI. I asked why I was never tested for the BRCA gene. My doctor had not considered it because I told her my mother did not have cancer; neither did my grandmothers, who both lived well into their mid-90s. But that was only half the story, since DNA comes from both parents. Later we learned it passed silently from our father's father. Our father was 84 years old. In his generation no one discussed breast or ovarian cancer with men. Those were "female issues," and taboo. My father wouldn't even allow us to tell him about it now. My sister and I were blindsided.

The MRI was inconclusive as scar tissue made it hard to read; but there was something there. The doctor said I could be monitored, or have another needle biopsy now, or wait and have another MRI in six months. The recommendation she leaned more towards was to have a double mastectomy. All these choices puzzled me and I was overwhelmed. I was dating Hunter exclusively and hoped to create a new life. I wanted to go out and enjoy the world; not go to the hospital! When would it be my time for a normal life?

I called my sister from the car to invite her to my "pity party," but she would have none of it. "You can't date when you're a corpse. I loved you when you didn't have breasts, and if this guy is a real man, he'll see your worth and love you no matter what. Grow a pair!" she said. The irony of that last part made us both laugh.

While on a dinner date that night, I was on edge. When Hunter asked what was wrong, I explained the BRCA gene, my increased risk of breast cancer, and the recommendation of preventive surgery. "If you're hearing -- run Forest, run! -- in your head, I get it," I said. "My husband was chronically ill and it's very challenging."

"Are you kidding me? I want to marry you!" Hunter said as he reached across the table to hold my hand. "When's the surgery?" He said grinning. "I've got your back." My sister was right. A real man won't run when the terrain gets rough. Hunter was ready to put on his boots and help me to kick cancer's butt.

I lost confidence in my original surgeon and looked for a new option. My sister pushed me to hurry up. "Act now, so your kids won't be orphans." I did my research and was introduced to two amazing specialists who operated as a team (Dr. Namnoum and Dr. Barber). My MRI was reviewed. I was counseled and informed that with my medical history it was advisable I take action as soon as possible. If they allowed me to wait six months, it could be considered malpractice. By planning my surgery I would avoid cancer; it would be less invasive; and I would have a better outcome.

I was still reluctant and afraid to go for the surgery, but it wasn't only my life it impacted. How could I ask my children to see me through chemotherapy? Hadn't they been through enough? I saw what my sister endured. It would be selfish of me to wait when I could stop cancer from happening. I arrived at the hospital at 5:30 a.m. As I waited, I silently prayed for my doctors and for God's protection of my children.

It was a very complicated 10-hour surgery, successfully accomplished by an expert team. My plastic surgeon made meticulous incisions at the areolas to retain the nipples and allow the breast surgeon to remove the potentially cancerous breast tissue. Precise incisions were made on my back, a flap of the latissimus muscle dissected, and tunneled around to my chest to create a support for a tissue expander for my reconstruction.

I was hospitalized nearly an entire week. Even with morphine I had pain. My armpits throbbed and I could not lift my arms. I was humbled to need assistance to do even simple things. I realized it was a small price to pay for a clean pathology and knowing I had finally dodged breast cancer.

I was discharged, and for weeks my chest was wrapped like a mummy. I had four wounds, each with a surgical drain that required constant attention. Pam, a college friend and nurse, was wonderful and flew in to provide skilled care. My recovery was a long 12-week process. Haley, who is such a loving and dedicated daughter, changed her college schedule. She commuted nearly two hours each way (to and from campus) several times a week to care for me. Thom, sensitive and compassionate, prepared meals and checked to make sure I wasn't in pain during the night. Shauna came over daily and organized friends' visits so I was never alone. Judy even washed my hair! I was not prepared for how difficult the recovery was. Friends drove me to weekly plastic surgeon appointments to have my expanders filled with saline. My sister came between her chemotherapy, kept me company and reinforced I made the right decision. I am so grateful for all the people who got me through it!

Once I regained my normal volume, I was scheduled for the next phase of reconstruction. A small incision was made in the breast folds. The tissue expanders removed, and state of the art implants actually being studied by the FDA inserted. Fat was transferred to give me a natural shape and feel. It was a much easier surgery. The results were amazing.

My sister timed it so she flew back to keep me company between cycles of her chemotherapy. I was more worried about her then myself. As another form of physical therapy, she taught me to crochet and we sat around happily chatting with balls of wool between us on my bed. I recovered beautifully and the strength and mobility returned to my arms. What a relief to say goodbye to hospitals and cancer surveillance and get back to living a happy life.

There was little reprieve. Only months after I recovered, my sister's cancer spread and she asked I fly back up to help her. It was as if we were little girls on the see-saw. When one was down, the other was up, and we took turns to support and lift one another, over and over again. That's what sisters do.

There was more surgery, infections, and a wait to get on a new chemotherapy. The uncertainty frightened her most. I stayed by her side day and night. During many of those nights we had conversations about the existence of God, the nature of God, and the purpose of God in our society. While it is important to respect that each person's spiritual journey is unique and unfolding, I felt time was getting away, and that this was a battle for her soul. It was my privilege that she confided in me, and I wanted to help her. Faced with death, she reaffirmed her beliefs. She expressed that she hoped she would be able to account for her sins, omissions, and mistakes, and when she faced her Maker, that He would appreciate she learned compassion. It was only her own cancer that gave her a better understanding of the world and creation. She still struggled with her faith but asked for prayer from me and from women in her church and in my church. I assured her God loved her and she was already forgiven. Cancer has a way of tilling the soil for faith to grow. She got strong again and we met in Philadelphia at the FORCE (Facing Our Risk of Cancer Empowered) hereditary cancer conference. We had our own agenda, to find a clinical trial. The forum provided access to medical, surgical, and radiation oncologists, research scientists, pharmaceutical executives, the FDA, and other women with ovarian and breast cancer. It gave us the latest information. I was inspired to be among BRCA cancer warriors and know we were part of a large community dedicated to improve patient outcomes. I was unaware of FORCE until after my surgeries. My sister found them in her research and she was the first to get involved. We were vocal patient advocates, and were approached to have our stories taped for a series of videos to raise awareness. We willingly agreed. I was later trained as a FORCE volunteer patient advocate.

Connections made at FORCE helped identify a compassionate care trial. I was proud that my sister made it a goal to not only help herself, but she advocated for inclusion of other women in the trial. This made her a hero to the other patients in her oncologist's office. During the experimental treatment, despite her suffering, she remained hopeful.

Everyone agreed that living with aggressive cancer for over three years was a miracle. The endurance and resilience she modeled was inspirational. We both learned the hard lessons of the difficulty of living with the uncertainty of long-term illness and recovery from repeated surgery. She asked me how Peter and I went through so many trials over such an extended period of time. I freely shared our secret: faith, family, and friends. God always sent the right people when we needed them most. I promised to stay with her for as long as she needed me. Ultimately, cancer spread throughout her abdomen, destroyed her digestive system, and flooded her lungs. The end was very difficult.

Always and forever my big sister, from the time she taught me to tie my shoes, to how she always courageously went first to blaze the trail. She continued to educate me and try to protect me all the days of her life. I loved my sister very much. She demonstrated grace as she selflessly educated me about hereditary cancer. She derived comfort and great satisfaction that she influenced me, and saw me through my lifesaving bilateral mastectomy. While she fought her own terminal cancer with everything she had, she was also determined to fight for me and the women she met on her journey. I am grateful for the love she showed. Because she pushed me to take action—I am done with breast cancer!

I know the BRCA floating around in my DNA may still trigger cancer in me; but I refuse to spend my time worrying about it. Today I volunteer with FORCE to use my life experiences to be a sister to someone else going through cancer. God brought me to this day for a reason, and I will trust Him.

I am thankful for my sister's life, though it was cut too short. I am appreciative our stories were videotaped, and that I have an opportunity to write about it, too. I share my story and faith openly. I raise awareness so someone else won't lose their sister. I am grateful our bond was restored. I am humbled God calls me to share our story of hope and redemption, and wish others will be blessed by it.

We never know when we will be called home. Life is a gift. Unconditional love is holy. I learned the lessons of forgiveness and I experienced the joy of serving others. Peter, my sweet husband, and my warrior sister each faced eternity with an admirable dignity and courage.

I will strengthen you and help you.
I will hold you up with my victorious right hand.
Isaiah 41:10

They encouraged me to move forward, not grieve and simply embrace life. In the midst of great suffering, I came to see death could be mercy. I thank God for this lesson, though it was so very painful. I also learned love transcends Heaven and earth. Nothing can destroy love. We are all called to keep shining the light. May their memories be a blessing.

Vanessa Brown

Age: 44

Georgia

6-Year Survivor/Thriver

ABOUT THE AUTHOR

Originally from Brooklyn, NY, Vanessa is the daughter of Fred and Florida Carlis. She is the proud mother of two children, Christina Carlis (25) and Amarkant Sukhan (18). Vanessa finds the most pleasure in hanging out with her family, especially vacationing together. She currently resides in McDonough, GA.

CHAPTER TWO

"I SHALL NOT DIE, BUT LIVE AND DECLARE THE WORKS OF THE LORD."

PSALMS 118:17 (KJV)

by Vanessa Brown

Vanessa, "I'm sorry, but your job has been eliminated!" That's what I was told June, 2009. What I thought was devastating news, potentially saved my life.

A couple of months before my job elimination I found a lump in my right breast. I wasn't at all alarmed because I had fibrocystic breasts and a lumpy breast wasn't something that was unusual for me. For weeks, I continued to check to see if the lump had gone away, but it didn't. When I lost my job and my medical insurance was going away, it prompted me to call my breast doctor that I had been seeing for a couple of years.

When I called, they gave me an appointment the next morning. The doctor ordered a sonogram so that he could get a picture of what was going on. He said to me, "Vanessa, this doesn't look normal, so I would like to biopsy some of the breast tissue. We can do it here in the office and we will have the results in a couple of days."

After the biopsy I went home to pack because my husband, Jerome, and my children, Christina and Amarkant, were going back to my hometown, Brooklyn, NY, for the 4th of July weekend. I was so excited to be going because I had not been there in a year. After arriving and settling in, the next day I received a call from the doctor informing me that my test results indicated that the lump in my breast was positive for cancer. I remember that phone call like it was yesterday. After I heard breast cancer, I didn't hear anything else the doctor said that day. It was like he was speaking another language that I did not understand.

I hung up the phone, gave my husband the news, and, of course, I cried in his arms. I immediately called my mother, as I always do, for any situation that I encountered. As I cried on the phone, she started praying. My husband whisked me outside because he didn't want my children to know what was going on, but, of course, my daughter felt that something was not right. She continued to ask me, "What's wrong Mommy?" I finally broke down and told her. My husband talked me through all of the emotions that I was feeling at the time, and he said, "We will get through this, we've been through a lot of adversity and we will beat this." My husband was born with sickle cell disease, and he had a couple of close calls himself. When he would be in the hospital for weeks and the doctors would only gave him a 50/50 chance to pull through a crisis, *God* always performed a miracle and he would walk out of the hospital against all the odds, so he knew the healing power of "God."

I carried on with my vacation in Brooklyn without ever crying or breaking down again. I was a little fearful of the unknown because no one in my family ever had breast cancer, so I didn't have anyone to talk to about it. On my return from New York, I was praying and listening to God's Word and heard Him say you need to fast. Fasting wasn't unusual for me because I had done a 40-day fast and drank water, eaten fruit, read my Bible and listened to the Word to feed my mind and body.

So I fasted for seven days on just liquids, so I could hear clearly from the Lord. I needed to make the right decisions about the protocol for my health, and I needed to know what *"God"* wanted me to do, not what "I" wanted to do.

I had a doctor's appointment the next day after I arrived home to discuss my options. My mother and husband accompanied me for the visit. The doctor stated that I had the best-case scenario for a breast cancer diagnosis. The cancer was "HER2 positive," and I could opt to have a lumpectomy or mastectomy. I knew that I didn't want to lose my breast, but I still tossed around the idea of having the mastectomy. My final decision was to have the lumpectomy, in which the surgeon makes an incision in the breast and removes the tumor, along with a small rim of normal tissue.

September, 2009, at 38 years old, I went into the hospital for outpatient surgery to remove the lump and one lymph node. The doctor only wanted to remove one node and test it during the surgery to make sure the cancer wasn't in the nodes, and it came back negative. I remember waking up and feeling really nauseous and even puking right after surgery. They sent me home the same day to recover. Surgery is never easy, no matter how minor it is, and I was feeling the after effects.

I was scheduled for a follow-up with my doctor to check my closed-suction drain bulb (removes fluids that build up on areas of the body after surgery) four days later, and I was told that the pathology report showed my margins were not "clear" (negative, or clean), which meant that cancer cells were seen at the outer edge of the tissue that was removed. The next day I was scheduled to go back into surgery to clear the margins. I was crushed!! The thought of having another surgery was disheartening. I didn't want to do this again. I prayed and asked God, why is this happening to me? I felt like I didn't have a choice; and if I wanted to be sure the cancer was gone, I had to have another surgery.

Less than a week after my first surgery, I was back at the hospital to do it all over again. I can't tell you how nervous I was. I was also pretty upset that I had to go back under the knife; I kept thinking, why didn't the doctor get this right the first time?

For the first surgery my daughter Christina came home from college to be there. She was on the basketball team and she took time away from practice and games to be by my side, but this time I insisted that she stay at school and that I would be fine. My mother, husband and son journeyed back with me to try this again, and it was a success. At my follow-up appointment I was told that the margins were now clear. The next step after recovering from surgery was to see an oncologist and to come up with a treatment plan. We spoke and she suggested seven weeks of radiation.

The oncologist was a very gentle person and she was a Believer. One of my prayers was answered. I asked God to surround me with doctors who believed in Him and heard His voice *clearly*. And I also wanted someone who had my best interest at heart, doctors that truly cared about their patients. After the visit with her, she asked me and my husband if it was okay if she prayed with us. We joined hands as she said a mighty prayer in her office that day. She prayed for me as well as my husband, and we left feeling good and positive about the care that I would receive as well as the treatment plan.

Several weeks had passed, and it was time for me to start the radiation—and I was so afraid. My husband drove me to the radiation treatment center and I didn't want to get out of the car. I signed myself in and went back to the car because I just didn't want to do it. At that moment, I had another breakdown, the second one since I received the diagnosis and surgery. All the emotions just came down on me all at once and I just couldn't go through with the treatments. I think I scared Jerome and he just didn't know what to do. The nurses that would administer the treatment came to the car. She shared with me her near-death story and she explained to me what would happen and ensured me that I would be just fine.

After about 20 minutes I went into the facility to receive my first radiation treatment and afterwards I thought…this isn't so bad, after all. But after five straight days of being radiated, I changed my tune! It drained all the energy that I had. I was so happy that I was still out of work because there was no way that I would have made it through a full day without having to sleep a few hours. My skin was also severely burned and it was very painful, but I kept pressing on.

On December 24, 2009, I received the last treatment and I was told that the cancer was gone and I could go on with my life. I also received news the same day that I was being rehired at my job. It was one of the best days ever.

Let's fast forward to March, 2013. I was just not feeling like myself. I can't really explain what it was, but I knew I just didn't feel good. I was also experiencing a lot of pain in my right side, shortness of breath, and a chronic cough that continued to get worse. At my place of employment they have a health center just for employees, and I decided to go see the doctor because I was progressively getting worse as the days and weeks passed. The doctor said that I had bronchitis, but she was concerned with the pain on my side and she thought it may be gall stones, so she scheduled me to have an x-ray at another facility.

The results showed that I had a pleural effusion. I had no idea what that was, and yet I still wasn't alarmed. She suggested that I go see an internal doctor right away.

Once again, I was feeling afraid. My daughter accompanied me to the appointment with this new doctor. She ordered me to have another x-ray and what she told me was a total shock. She said the cancer may have come back!! How could that be? I had just seen the breast doctor and had an exam and a mammogram a couple of weeks earlier and all the results were negative. I was diligent to keep my appointments with him every six months, so I was confused when she told me that it may have come back.

28

I broke down. I tried not to cry but I just had to release it, for just a moment. I told my daughter, no worries; I'm going to be fine! We walked to the car and I called my mother. Again, she prayed as I cried.

The doctor ordered me to have a thoracentesis. This is a procedure that is done on an outpatient basis, and a needle is inserted in between your ribs and your back to reach the pleural space between the chest wall and lung. The pleural fluid is removed through a syringe. The fluid is sent to the lab and tested to see if cancer cells are present.

A week later I was told that cancer cells were present in the fluid and that the cancer had metastasized. What is that I asked? It means that the cancer had left the breast and spread to other parts of my body. What do you mean it left the breast? I didn't know how that could happen. I was so confused and angry at myself because I thought that just seeing the breast doctor I was doing my part to stay cancer free. I didn't know that I was supposed to continue to see the oncologist. I didn't educate myself, and that's why I was angry. I was ordered to go back to see the oncologist. She wanted me to have a PET scan right away. But before I could get the scan, I had to go back to the hospital for my third thoracentesis, because the fluid kept building up in the pleural cavity on my right side and I was unable to walk a few feet without becoming out of breath. This time there were some complications. The needle punctured my lung and it collapsed. I had to be admitted to the hospital to be monitored; all the while the fluid was building up again, so I had to get a chest tube inserted to drain it. Having the chest tube was very uncomfortable because it was painful. At night in the hospital bed I would pray and talk to God. I wanted Him to strengthen and comfort me because I didn't know why this was happening to me, but I would soon get my answer.

After seven days, I was released from the hospital. By this time I had lost almost 25 pounds, I was weak and deteriorating, but I still talked to God every day. One night I lay prostrate before the Lord and I cried and begged Him not to take me away from my son Amar. He was just 16 and about to graduate from high school and he still needed me, and I wanted to be here for him and his children and his children's children.

My daughter Christina drove me to get the PET scan and before we could get home the doctor called and said the cancer was in the pelvic area. I asked, not the lungs? She said no. So I want you to see a gynecological oncologist. I went there and she said that the cancer was in my lungs, pelvic cavity and pleural cavity, and I need to be on chemotherapy immediately.

My mom and I went back to the oncologist and her exact words to me were, "I can only prolong your life." My faith was being tested, but I stood on God's word that I was going to be healed, and I didn't waiver. We left that office and we immediately took action!

James 5:14 says, "Is any sick among you? Let him call for the elders of the church; and let him pray over him anointing him with oil in the name of the Lord." My mother Florida, my Aunt Van and Sister Linda of the church did just that. They prayed with me and anointed me with oil. All the while I was draped with a prayer shawl. After about 30 minutes of prayer, I was in tears, because it was so powerful, and I felt the Holy Spirit there in the room with us!

I also called a colleague to get some advice, because I had been getting the runaround from the doctors here in Atlanta and after almost two months from being diagnosed, I still had not received treatment. A few days later I was flown to a cancer treatment center in Chicago. June, 2013, I started on two different types of heavy rounds of chemo. Although I was experiencing many side effects from the medication, I still came to work. It was very difficult at times, but I put a smile on my face and remained happy and thankful that I was still alive.

A co-worker approached me and told me how good I looked, despite all that I was going through. She had some very serious medical issues herself and had just returned to work. She said to me that I inspired her to get up and get out of the bed every day, because if I could come to work a couple of days after flying back from Chicago and having heavy doses of chemotherapy every three weeks, then she could too. I was in tears; I didn't know that this journey was helping someone else. And at that moment I received my answer.

As the months passed, my brief encounters with many others would further confirm that this wasn't about me—it was about helping others. I was a vessel, to inspire, encourage, motivate and help others to build their faith, and to show that GOD is HEALER.

I continue to pray daily and confess God's Word; HIS word will heal your body. Once it is conceived in the Spirit, it will permeate in the body, and I am a LIVING witness! It's been over two years since the second diagnosis, and today I am cancer free. HALLELUJAH!

Dedicated to my beloved husband, Jerome Brown, Sr. (March 31, 1969 – February 20, 2015).

TeMaya Eatmon

Age: 38
Georgia
Two-Year Survivor/Thriver

ABOUT THE AUTHOR

Since TeMaya's diagnosis and journey, she has begun advocacy work around public policy and research. Her work is particularly centered on healthcare disparities amongst minorities and young women. In an effort to achieve this, TeMaya is focused on doing her part to change the face of breast cancer, so people see that you can THRIVE after cancer.

TeMaya currently resides in Atlanta with her husband, JaMichael. She enjoys traveling, cooking, spa days, and spending time with close family and friends.

CHAPTER THREE

THROUGH MY EYES

by TeMaya Eatmon

My story begins on July 25, 2012, when I married a special man, JaMichael. It was a true modern-day courtship; and life was good. Shortly after returning from our honeymoon, I began having a discharge from my breast. I scheduled an appointment with my OB/GYN for my annual exam and to discuss this issue. After talking with my doctor and getting the exam results returned, I was sent for a CT scan to check out my pituitary gland. After the test, I got a call that there was nothing abnormal, but at my next PCP visit, to possibly have prolactin levels checked.

Well in the interim, I had to go back to the OB/GYN and life went from being good to really good because we were expecting our first child, and that's the reason for the breast discharge. We were truly overjoyed! We decide to get through the first trimester before we told the masses. But being an only child, I had to tell my mother. Her only child, her first grandchild, and, yes, she was over the moon.

At our second appointment after finding out we were going to be parents, we were pulled to the side by the doctor to let us know that due to some large fibroids, the baby was about two weeks behind developmentally and we should be prepared for the worse.

We agreed that we would prepare by praying first, and then by speaking life into our baby each and every day. We played music and read books. JaMichael began rubbing my stomach and listening for the heartbeat each night before bed. In our eyes we were experiencing a piece of heaven through this experience.

My breast discharge had turned bloody and an appointment was scheduled to do a urine test later that week; however, I never made that appointment. Because, early on the morning of October 19, 2012, I began experiencing horrible abdomen pains and when I went to the bathroom, I knew. I was having a miscarriage!

Upon making it in to the doctor for the medical/professional confirmation, I asked if the bloody discharge would now go away, and upon my showing her the nursing pads I had been wearing; I was immediately sent to the breast center. Just having to go at all was frightening enough, and then realizing you were the only person under 40 in the whole center, even worse. All types of thoughts began to creep into my head, and all I could begin doing was calling on the name of Jesus.

I endured a mammogram and they had me endure an ultrasound as well. After I finished both, I went to the nurse navigator's office where I was told I would need a biopsy. I scheduled for the first available, which was three days later. My nurse navigator was there with me, held my hand and made sure I had recovered enough to go home. You see, I didn't tell anyone about this because I was convinced there was no need for excitement. It was just a biopsy. The next day I got the call; it was benign, but it was a large enough tumor that it needed to be removed. I figured I would have it done when I was scheduled to have my fibroids removed. Everyone agreed it was a super-solid plan.

My OB/GYN was going to remove my fibroids and found a breast surgeon to remove my tumor. I was going to be set. I was going to have my fibroids removed so I would be able to experience that piece of heaven again; or so I thought. I realized that we make plans and God laughs because it's not part of His plan, or inevitably our destiny. So even though things didn't quite turn out like I planned, I know I am blessed and know that, through my eyes, there were constant trials and tribulations I experienced but He never left me. Through my eyes and with His grace, I have a testimony.

Life Changes

Dec. 14, 2012 7:41 p.m.

Today my life changed. After being out of the hospital one whole day; I received a call from my breast surgeon who I only anticipated ever seeing one time, or at least not until I was 40. The pathology report came back and I have Stage Zero breast cancer. All I could think about was "wow," my life changed in the blink of an eye.

Decisions

Jan. 16, 2013 9:34 p.m.

Today we got the pathology report from Dr. BB, and unfortunately the margins were not where they needed to be in order for the lumpectomy to be a success. We have to make a decision as to whether or not we want to try for another lumpectomy or if we are going to go ahead with the mastectomy. The doctor's recommendation is for the mastectomy, due to my age, but it will be our decision.

Full Day

Jan. 20, 2013 8:17 p.m.

Yesterday was a truly busy day for me. It started with a sorority meeting, followed by lunch with my good friend since college, and dessert with one of my dearest sister friends. I truly needed to push myself, as it was the first weekend (time period), I had been out of the house for substantial length of time since the myomectomy. I was beat, but it gave me some much-needed normalcy. These days, normalcy is more like a dream.

Reality

Jan. 21, 2013 10:15p.m.

Today I visited a reconstruction surgeon. Initially, I wasn't impressed with the two pictures of African Americans on her site, so had some reservations about leaving something this traumatic and life changing up to this doctor. At the end of the appointment I felt a sense of comfort. However, in reviewing all my options reality hit. I will have to take some medication (Tamoxifen) that will prevent the cancer from reoccurring. *However,* I will not be able to get pregnant for at least 2 years. Reality #2 is that my choice for a mastectomy affects how much time I will stay in the hospital, as well as the overall recovery. Reality #3 is that this will not be an easy journey. In moments like this, I was definitely glad that my mother was there and I can see that I am probably going to need support for the majority of my appointments.

Anniversary

Jan. 25, 2013 5:55 a.m.

Today is my 6-month wedding anniversary and it has truly been the complete opposite of what I could have ever imagined. I have no choice but to believe in His word, as something better and beyond my wildest dreams has to come out on the other side. We went to visit my doctor and got a better grasp and understanding on everything. So, we will be going with a unilateral mastectomy. Definitely hard to come to grips with, but when you choose life, those decisions are oftentimes more complex than one would think.

Here's the deal: my breast are so dense that MRI and mammogram could not detect the path of the cancer, as typically in DCIS cancer there would be calcium traces and the technology would detect it. Once this detection is made, they are able to path the cancer and establish a definitive treatment plan. Without this knowledge, treatment is extremely hard to properly plan for. That presents a problem for longevity; hence, the reason for our decision.

Friends

Jan. 29, 2013 6:08 a.m.

I have truly been overwhelmed by the love I have received from my closest friends. They have given me and JaMichael an outpouring of love. Even though I have been slow in returning calls and my text responses have been slower or gone unanswered for days, they understand and just check in with JaMichael. However, I have a few "regular" calls that I expect and even when I'm down, I try to find the energy because in the end I know they are going to leave me with a smile.

My family has been remarkable as always, and my mother's love during this period makes me want to be a mother myself even more. I am also blessed and grateful that she has friends that regularly check up on her as well, considering I believe she is having a harder time than I am.

Long, Long Week

Feb. 3, 2013 9:16 a.m.

This was my first full week back at work and my body feels it. My nurse navigator stated that I healed extremely well and fast from the myomectomy, but in reality I had no choice. I had no choice because I had to prepare my mind and body for the fight against breast cancer. I had so many appointments shortly following my surgery (about two per week) that I didn't truly rest the four weeks that I was supposed to, and now my body feels it. So this week, working nine-hour days (to make up for the days and hours I will need to be out or leave work on intermittent FMLA) really kicked my butt. There were things I wanted to do, but the energy just wasn't there. I did cook made-from-scratch soup for JaMichael, but wanted to do more for him. I actually made it to the mall to get a co-worker a birthday gift, and enjoyed it for a minute, but it became a task going from one end of the mall to the other. There were some other things that I wanted to look at, but my energy was like—you better save it for the drive home. Actually, all that depleted energy did was roll over to Saturday, and while I was planning on meeting one of my "big sisters" for lunch, I just didn't have it in me. I am doing minimal activity today as tonight is the big game and we were invited over one of my best girlfriend's home for a party, and I know I will be there with her family and we always have a ball, so I want to reserve that energy. It is my prayer that my energy increases as the weeks go by, as my next surgery is right around the corner; March 27th. . . .

Too Much

Feb. 6, 2013 6:34 p.m.

Today was the day for my genetics testing and MRI biopsy. The day started fine; work for half a day and then to Piedmont for the MRI. Piedmont is where things took a major shift. After going through the MRI for about 45 minutes, they pulled me out and despite my prayers that nothing would be found, the contrast saw two small masses in the right breast, and as they were reading the coordinates from one machine the other machine could not capture it. And, so (20 minutes of them trying to get it and calling in the vendor for one of the devices), they put me back in the MRI machine. About 10 minutes back in I got so sick and nauseated that I had to get an emergency stop. It was truly too much. I hadn't eaten, as that was a requirement for my doing the genetic testing. I opted for it to be late in the day so that I could go to work and not utilize more of my

FMLA time than necessary. So after 2.5 hours, I ended up in tears, pain, and just wishing this was all over. But it wasn't. I headed to my genetic testing 30 minutes late (my nurse navigator called ahead to tell them I would be late). I learned more about genetics testing than I thought I would ever care to know. I was drained and just wanted to actually finish something today. I wanted to do my part to help get the answers about my disease. I wanted to be strong. I wanted to be able to tell my mother and JaMichael everything went well so that they could be proud of me and see my strength.

The Big Chop

Feb. 9, 2013 7:09 a.m.

Well, last night after two months of not seeing my fabulous hair stylist at Too Groovy, I made it back to officially experience "THE BIG CHOP." Granted, my hair had already significantly fallen out, but some of it was still holding on. Each morning I would try to do something with it, but there were too many patches to accomplish much. So after rocking my scarves for the past month, I decided that as I embrace my reality, I had to embrace my new hair. JT (my stylist) sent me a text with the India Arie quote from "I Am Not My Hair," and so my hair was shaved. I enjoyed being in the salon, as that had been a weekly ritual for me since getting engaged last year and growing my hair for my wedding. However, I had a range of feelings from *ashamed* (when I took my scarf off) to *curious* when she started the cut; to being *empowered* when I walked out. The part that really got to me was, as she cut and styled me, there were other clients of other stylist with long, flowing hair just looking in shock. It made me wonder if they just thought my hair was so damaged and that I had to start over, or did they know and feel sorry for me? I will never know the answer to those questions, but I do know that *I am not my hair*. Who knows, maybe it will grow back with thick curls and, as it gets longer, I will be able to rock long flowing Beyoncé curls with/out a weave or a wig ☺

My Valentine's

Feb. 14, 2013 7:39 p.m.

Well, my Valentine's this year was quite different than last year. Last year when I celebrated, I received an appointed position in the Junior League, and then, most importantly, I got engaged. This year, I believe, was just as great, as we celebrated the Saturday before with our marriage ministry at church; had dinner a day earlier because I was going to a retreat for Leadership Buckhead on Valentine's evening. I celebrated the day of with my staff and was pleasantly surprised to receive two dozen of the most beautiful red roses from my husband prior to my leaving. But what a difference a year makes.

This was my first Valentine's as a wife, and as we headed to my surprise dinner location on the 13th, JaMichael had quite a different conversation with me. He asked me about my friends and was I being a good friend. Not quite the conversation I was intending on having as we celebrated our first Valentine's Day. I informed him that I journal via the Internet, so that my friends and family can see what is going on, even when I don't answer/return a phone call. He stated that the ones that I thought enough of to share this site can only find out what is going on via Internet—interesting.

I then shared my argument/justification, but my husband LOVES me, and so I knew there was something more. He shared that, granted, while I'm on this journey and going through it, that those closest to me are also going through it—and while this method is truly a great tool that I need to do better, that my friends should have access to hear my voice, even if only for a minute on those bad days. So, considering it was Ash Wednesday and we prepare for the Lenten season, I have committed to answering the phone more and making more of an effort to return calls, because without them it would be a lot harder. So on the day of love, I am in the woods on my retreat; thinking about all my family and friends on the journey with me, and I all I can say is: Love you to pieces!

Simplicity and Balance

Feb. 17, 2013 7:58 a.m.

I attended my Leadership Buckhead Retreat and the theme was "Simplicity and Volume." Considering what is going on with me in my life, this session was most appropriate. There were so many reflections on the simple things we did as a child. The activities were thought-provoking: such as packing only a shoebox for the weekend, filled with the things you figured you had to have in order to make-do for two days; doing your own personal "last lecture"; and writing down your day and assigning times to them; having to learn something about one individual that made you stop and do a double-take that you didn't already know; and doing silent walks.

My diagnosis on December 14th forced me to stop where I was and adjust. I adjusted to what my reality would be—uncertainty; more doctor appointments than the law allows; more tears; and a halt on a new job that was to start the day I was on the operating table in January. Balance: *HA!* Simple: a joke! But, over time, I have had no choice but to find balance; as without it, things become so overwhelming. I have had to look at the simple things and find joy in them. Doing this (along with prayer) has changed my life.

I was reminded that, even if I have to "schedule" time, I need to be more diligent for "me-time" and fellowship time with those that mean the most. I was also reminded that everyone does not need, or deserve, a front row seat in my life. However, through the activities, many of my peers in the program were amazed of the trials I had been undergoing, and I was told that my story was truly an inspiration for the changes they needed to make for their lives. I told them I wanted to be the face they thought of when they thought of breast cancer, and

41

that I am going to be alright, but that your life can change in an instant, so take time to be clear about *who* and *what* means the most, stop making excuses for the dreams you have and just do them, and, most importantly, enjoy the smallest things. I was touched by the impact and the session where a peer had to speak about me and how she said I have been the reason she had already begun to look at things from a different lens and would have never thought I had breast cancer because I have remained upbeat and positive. All I could say was, "BUT God."

We had Derreck Kayongo come and speak, and at that moment I had an "Ah-ha moment." He stated that, sometimes despite our understanding, things will align themselves, and it is up to us to determine which course and what we plan to do with what has been placed before us. It just confirmed what I thought about during my silent walk and looked up to the heavens. God will give you a sign/confirmation, and I received and embraced mine.

Seattle

Feb. 21, 2013 9:02 p.m.

I made it to Seattle for my first breast cancer conference, and all I can say is *WOW*. It was strange because, as I arrived on Thursday, I believe I expected everyone to know I was part of the conference and just be super welcoming, but they weren't. I mean, at the end of the day I had no pink on, and I guess I assumed they would associate my new no-hairstyle as an automatic cancer sorority brand. So, I decided to just enjoy the very late night with a burger and fries and some Scandal. I have a busy day tomorrow.

Pink

Feb. 22, 2013 2:00 p.m.

Okay, so I just sent my BFF a text to let her know that I think I am at her sorority's boule. Honestly, I love fuchsia (as many know) but this pink thing is truly overwhelming. Overwhelming in the sense that now this is real! I am part of one of the largest "sororities" that no one actually volunteers for. At a time when I should feel so empowered, I actually feel alone and scared. I met one survivor who is here with her mom and I wanted my mother to be here with me, and then in the next instant I was glad I was here alone because I was "exuding" my mother with strength and courage. I talked to Ms. Rachel—the mom—and got some truly deep insight from the point of view of a mom. All I can say is, it was a lot; when they say you are on the journey with other people, you really are—but because I have been so consumed, I don't always notice it.

My new friend, Jacqueline, is from New Mexico and is Latina. We have the same type of breast cancer, but hers was invasive (Stage 2), where mine was not. It's another reason to truly thank God and all those around me who pray with and for me. Her story could have been mine, but by His grace, my story is different. She has already undergone her mastectomy but had to do delayed reconstruction due to chemo and radiation. Understanding her journey has truly helped me understand, and feel God on this journey. I haven't met anyone else, as it appears many people are regulars and have been to the conference several times and keep returning with the friends they made over the years. I'm headed to my advocacy program, so I will see what that has in store for me as I realize this testimony is not just for me.

Information Overload

Feb. 23, 2013 10:38 p.m.

Today was filled with so-o-o much information. The day started at 8:30 and went 12 hours strong with a dance party starting soon. I'm so worn out, but it is a good worn out. The day was filled with sessions that are relevant and gave different perspectives. It started with an overview of the disease and where research is headed. I then went to an intimacy session, as I have had some personal struggles, and felt being amongst women going through what I am could be beneficial. I just want my husband to still be attracted to me, but in order for that to happen, I need to feel attractive. Afterwards, I was off to a reconstruction session that has really made me need to talk with my surgeons as well as continue to find other options. I have to put the money to the side and make a quality-of-life decision. I know I have to have a mastectomy because I can only have so many anniversaries before I can't have kids, and JaMichael and I have decided to try one last time, so this choice allows this. But while I have done my research, there is so much more out there. I have gotten information on a plethora of programs, so much so that it will probably take a week to go through everything—exactly why I came. While it has been a bit overwhelming, I have more tools, access, and information to ensure my QOL is optimal as I beat this disease and fight for it to never return.

25

Feb. 24, 2013 2:18 a.m.

While everyone here at the conference is on the journey, I realized tonight that I am blessed. I am blessed that, at the age of 25, my life could have been considered ideal. I had a good job; made good money; was engaged; had great friends; travelled the world; and my only cares were fashion related, and the corporate ladder. I had late-night appetizers with a group of ladies who were between 24-29 years old and all were two or more years into survivorship. They all talked about the range of emotions and the support or lack of. They discussed how friends and lovers walked away. They shared deep, intimate details. They shared their struggles. They shared how life was interrupted by stupid cancer. One young lady even told me how I was so lucky. My words to her were how brave and strong she was. It made me think about the plan God has for me: but know that this journey gives you an opportunity to begin again. My next 25 years will be better the second time around because I will be cancer free.

It's Complicated!

Mar. 9, 2013 7:26 a.m.

Well, since returning from the conference, most of my spare time has been consumed with researching doctors, filling out paperwork and trying to get appointments, and once that is achieved going to appointment after appointment. It has drained me to the point that I have been asleep just about every night by 8:30-9 p.m. (unheard of for me, as midnight is typically my time). I have to do this after attending the conference and discussion with my nurse navigator about my top three "take-backs"; Quality of Life, my journey is my journey, and no regrets. So, the no regrets resonated with me the most because my Granny use to always tell me that when you are making big decisions, decisions with large impacts/consequences, you should make the ones that will give you no regrets.

I can't say that if I had to make the decision today, that I would not have any regrets, and this decision is too big. So, I've found my own medical team that I want to "interview" and compare their diagnosis and treatment plans. I visited a surgical oncologist who stated I have been through a lot, and then stated my understanding of what was going on needed to be extremely clear. The doctor went on to say that, while my situation is complicated, it can be handled, and I can be cured. I can be a survivor without recurrence. So the decision I make has to be the right decision because it impacts the rest of my life.

Barely

Mar. 21, 2013 10:41 p.m.

Today I attempted the MRI biopsy for the second time. I had to have the procedure done at another location, as there was difficulty with Piedmont willing to schedule my appointment because I previously had a surgery scheduled, and the doctor's office wasn't willing to cancel until he returned from vacation. The bigger problem is there was only one date available before I go to single insurance. Insurance is huge, as each appointment consists of co-pay and possibly some additional out-of-pocket. If you have two insurances, one's out-of-pocket is minimal. So, considering I have been on a "tour" of doctors the past couple of weeks, I had a facility that was willing to do the procedure today.

I barely made it. MRI biopsy is about a two-hour process that involves you lying face down, and an actual shortened MRI being run, and then the doctor has to review the images and then find the site. So, at about 1:45, you are about to give up but, God. . . He placed a radiation tech in the room to massage my arm, which felt so weak that I actually reached for the ball to stop the procedure; but she wouldn't let me. She talked…she rubbed me. She did everything to contain me so I could get it done. I had taken my meds, but they seemed to be wearing off. She told me she wasn't going to let me quit. By then the doctor was ready for the actual biopsy, and it was probably the most pain I had received during this journey. Barely! But I did it, and when I finished, the radiation tech thanked God when I thanked her for pulling me through. These are the experiences that I hope no one reading this, or anyone they love, has to ever go through.

Finally

Apr. 12, 2013 11:12 p.m.

It has been awhile, but there has been so much going on in regards to my treatment and medical team overall. I have learned so much during this journey. I learned that the staff in a doctor's office can make or break a doctor. (I think I'm going into consulting after this experience.) I learned that knowing your benefits as far as insurance is essential. I learned that finding the "right" medical team for you is very similar to finding the right mate to marry. I know why people often have attitudes when they have more than one doctor's appointment, but understand why senior citizens are so patient at their doctor's appointments.

So finally, I have my medical team confirmed. I will be using Dr. JA as my breast surgeon and Dr. DA (I had previously removed names since she only used initials),"The Boob Fairy," as my reconstruction surgeon. I will continue to use Dr. WB as my medical oncologist. I will have to get a new nurse navigator but GS promised she would still be by my side ☺ I will be receiving care through the Women's Center at Northside and will have my accommodations on the breast cancer floor. You know, it is really sad that there is actually a full floor where only breast cancer patients are housed. Things need to change. There needs to be a cure, antidote, something! I chose this team because, for me, the staff and the feeling that I got when I left, when I've called, when I've been at their offices, has been one of relief, one that made me feel as though God Himself chose them. As one of the survivors told me, make your decision and own it, and don't question it because it is your journey. I plan on doing just that.

Cancer Patient

Apr. 13, 2013 5:39 p.m.

Well, I have decided to be a cancer patient and not super woman. What I mean by this is that I will be taking a month off prior to my surgery May 21st, as I need to be physically and mentally fit, and the latter is almost near impossible to do being employed at KS and dealing with everyone else's issues. I plan on going to the Cancer Wellness Center and doing some things to just get my mind off the surgery and live in the moment. I want to be the best wife that I can be during this time, as JaMichael will be my main caregiver through this journey and this time last year he would have never thought that as he approached his one-year anniversary that his wife would have breast cancer. So, I want to make sure he enjoys his wife to the fullest and show him how important he is to me, and in my life. I realized that this is such a major event in my life that, regardless of waking up with breast cancer, I have to be mentally ready. I'm going to take some time and get everything together, for life as I know it ends May 21, 2013. I will be restarting the rest of my life and it can only get better. I have breast cancer now, but as Dr. CJ tells me every week when she works in my office.   .by His stripes I am healed! I believe and receive it!

Doing Right

May 5, 2013 10:28 a.m.

So since my last update, I was supposed to be taking the month off to just be a cancer patient and that didn't happen. Even though one of the doctors (CH) and the executive leadership at my job are as close to I ever want to get to the devil, I had to do what was best for me. I have to repeat several scriptures each morning but I know that financially, I needed to work as long as I possibly could. I am going to do somewhat right and this Friday is my last day at KS (paperwork is in and signed off on). I am going to attend a couple of events prior, because I will miss several special moments: our 10-month anniversary dinner, my girlfriend's wedding, two girlfriends' EJ and JB's, birthdays (Geminis always celebrate together), and being able to be surrounded by friends and family on my birthday.

SIDENOTE: This will be the first time since I moved back to Atlanta that I won't be able to have some type of small gathering for my birthday. Yes, I did tell JaMichael I wanted a party, but he informed me that I would be less than four weeks out of the hospital and that wasn't happening. However, I came up with different scenarios; but then it hit me! My mother will probably still be at our house or coming by to stay with me while he is at work, so I guess I'm going to do right. Not to mention, I have to reserve my strength for DC in July for my sorority's Centennial event. I know if I don't take it easy and heal like I should, JaMichael is going to be looking at me with a crooked eye on letting me go. Do you know how long I have been anticipating this day? Since January 22, 2000. Yes, I am going to do right leading up to the surgery, so that it goes seamlessly after the surgery, so that I can heal properly, and until I get the two thumbs-up because I want to see Dr. DA and Dr. JA as little as possible.

The Countdown Begins

May 16, 2013 8:12 a.m.

So, I'm five days out from surgery and there are so many emotions. I go from excitement to anxiety. I am trying to keep fear as much out of it is as possible. I've been doing pretty well with that aspect, as I have been super busy this week. This was my first week off work and, boy, do I wish I had taken last week as well. JaMichael informed me I had events on the calendar every day this week…from support group to visiting my wonderful hair stylist. Yes, even with the little bit I have I still enjoy visiting the salon, and my stylist doesn't treat me as a cancer patient because I only have a little bit of hair on my head (natural hair salon bonus…love the Too Groovy Team). I have a Cancer Wellness program planned for today that was recommended by one of the ladies from the Young Survival Coalition support group later this morning, and then it will be on to my Leadership Buckhead graduation. This will be a fun and exciting time this evening for me because JaMichael will be able to meet many of the people that I have talked about and developed relationships with that will inevitably last for many years to come. This was truly a great experience, as many of these people I would have never met without this program, but they have so fulfilled my life and made it easier for me to share my story.

Then Friday is somewhat relaxation day minus grocery shopping, a stop by Kinko's, and then Marriage Ministry meeting. Saturday will be filled with my sweet, sweet Sorors (and if the meeting goes on too long, I will exit stage left…smile), then lunch with some of my KS co-workers (actually, just 1 present and 1 past), then dinner with one of my support group ladies (I missed that meeting, so we are meeting pre-surgery for encouragement). And so I guess JaMichael was correct in saying my schedule was busy, but it so keeps my mind off of the fear and any other negatives the devil will try to slip in on me. It's my hope to truly log each day leading up to my big day.

4 Days and Counting

May 17, 2013 10:22 p.m.

Wow…today was the four-day countdown, and WOW. I woke up today and, of course, everyone goes to the bathroom first (maybe TMI…) and when I went to wash my hands there was a note on the mirror. It was taken from a Leadership Buckhead skit, and I had to follow the Leadership Road to a surprise. The road was designed with pink gumballs and led to a pink Camicakes box with a wonderful strawberry cupcake …what a wonderful small thing to wake up to. I started some cleaning and then off to the grocery store, taking in every activity that is so often taken for granted and knowing that for six weeks even the simplest things may need to be overlooked so that I can completely and properly heal. I made it back in to get my assessment call from the hospital, and then everything changed.

All I had been preparing for is about to get REAL. The only thing that kept me calm was that the nurse emphasized how they would take care of me in the hospital and that she knew I would do well because she could hear the strength in my voice. The confirmation came when she said she would pray for me. A stranger praying for your healing and recovery is such a powerful thing. I think that is the reason that I am not too frantic. I was given even more peace as JaMichael and I attended our Marriage Ministry meeting and the subject was on keeping the bond. We were challenged to do something within the two weeks, and so JaMichael, being himself, said Sunday we would be doing our bonding activity because it is important to us both and it would be awhile before we could do something together; icing on the cake, and I thank God for him.

The Last 2

May 20, 2013 7:31 a.m.

The last 2 days have been extremely busy, time consuming, tiring, but oh so much fun and so needed. So, just a rundown starting with Saturday, sorority meeting then on to lunch with KS co-workers, then a stop off at Kinko's before heading to Wahoo Grill. I was able to celebrate with another survivor and see the love her friends have for her and how they are taking the journey with her, and then finally a stop at Camp Creek Marketplace to meet Ms. Fran to pick up my cake. Did I mention all this started at 9:15 a.m., and I returned to my house at 9:38 p.m.; yes, running for 12 hours....so praise the Lord JaMichael was heading out to an impromptu bachelor party, so I had the house to myself ☺ I really needed that! So that leads to Sunday, and it started with 7:15 a.m. church service. It was not an option for me going to church because, regardless of how tired or weak I may have felt, I knew that His Word would be what I need to get me through. So, it just so happened to be Senior Day—meaning senior citizen— and , honestly, I was like bedside Baptist may have been the ticket for me. But, Minister Hall preached, and if ever there was a stand in for Pastor Oliver, he's it. A phenomenal sermon, he ended with the story of Caleb slaying three giants at 85, and how David remembered that story when it was time for him to slay Goliath. The point was, if an 85-year-old could slay three giants, why couldn't a 17-year-old slay one, and then my picture in my Bible slid (it's me and my Granny the last time we went out together in October, 2009), and all I could think about was what she endured, and then I was, like, "Cancer-- bring it...I can defeat it because her spirit is with me"; shift to thought Number 2. . .my goddaughters and my niece are depending on me so they don't have to ever endure this disease and the pain. And, so I wept tears of joy in that moment and left filled with peace about my decision. So the devil will try to steal your joy at any time.

And once I arrived home, a full migraine came on, and I can only take Tylenol until surgery, but it's preferred you take nothing a week prior. Not to mention, my family and a few girlfriends were coming to cast my breast. I took the Tylenol and JaMichael made me breakfast and let me sleep for an hour and then I was ready. The devil was busy because it stormed, flooded, and hailed for hours and there were power outages and I began to feel like maybe the casting prior to surgery wasn't going to happen. . .BUT, God. My family showed up a little off schedule, but they came through the storms from Nashville, and my other girlfriend called to make sure it was a go; it all just came together. I was truly overjoyed. Of course, we had to watch the video for the casting multiple times, but the ladies worked together to get it completed. It turned out beautifully. I shared with them the procedure and what is going to happen on Tuesday. When I finished, they circled me in prayer. While they prayed for me I was thanking God for them. It was cake time and then everyone slowly departed. JaMichael and I had a date/assignment from Marriage Ministry, but the weather postponed that, and so we had a quiet evening at home.

Less Than 8 Hours

May 20, 2013 11:00 p.m.

I have less than 8 hours before we check into the hospital. I am up trying to stay up as late as possible so that once the anesthesia kicks in. I can be somewhat at a natural state of sleep. Today was much more relaxed than I initially planned and anticipated. I woke up and did some minimal cleaning, took a light nap, and met my aunt and cousin for lunch. While I was going to be going 100 mph, my aunt and cousin stepped in and stated that is what they were here to do. Many of the survivors stated that was what you need to do; so, I did, and all I did was take Dr. SA (my therapist) some cake and then back home to wait for my massage and a late dinner with JaMichael. In between, I got an overwhelming amount of calls and texts with prayers and thoughts that are going to be the thing to get me through. I couldn't imagine going through this without the support and love from friends and family. So, I will be off line for a couple of days. Thank you for being on the journey with me and keep me in your prayers because, at 11:30 a.m.

tomorrow, my life will change forever.

Road to Recovery

May 26, 2013 10:54 a.m.

I am now on the road to recovery. I can truly say it has been a journey and without the prayers and continuous uplifting of close friends and family, I don't know how I would have made it. I am truly blessed to have you in my life. While the surgery was a success, there was a brief moment of uncertainty. I have to say, when you have to fight to live, you have to have a reason to LIVE. I actually coded after my procedure and saw my Granny's face, and she said, "Maya, it's not time," as there is still work for you to do. In that moment I gave everything I had in order to just live. So many questions run through your head, like why did you bring me through this only for me to not come out? Why me? Why now? Was this the only impact I was supposed to have, am I really leaving a legacy? I mean, the questions just continue to flow and fear begins to settle in. Honestly, words can't adequately express how I felt. It was overwhelming. The only thing I could think about was JaMichael and my mother and how God doesn't put more on you than you can bear, and I knew me not coming out on the other side would be detrimental to them both; but God had also spoken to me in a voice that gave me peace to let me know all I had to do was FIGHT....and I fought like I was in the ring with the best of them...Mayweather, Ali, Tyson, and Holyfield. I did it, and I have a testimony!!

Something that had been in my spirit for weeks before yet resonates clearly now.... Fight for what matters most. Family and true friends matter the most, peace of mind, finding joy in each new day.

So for my cousin, who drove alone from Michigan so her mom could support my mother.. . .that matters...to two sister friends God specifically put on the journey with me, who took time off their jobs and away from their families. . .that matters. . .to my BFF, who traveled from DC to be here with me when I was released from the hospital. . .my girlfriends who fought the storms before to celebrate me. . .that is what matters most, girlfriends who despite their own obligations took time out to celebrate *me*. . .true game- changer and life-changer. So, my life is different and better despite it all. I sincerely thank and love you for the support you have given me, JaMichael, my family, and each other. I look forward to celebrating each birthday (I understand the American Cancer Society's campaign now☺), and each anniversary of being cancer free.

Roller Coaster

May 31, 2013 8:23 p.m.

It's been ten days since my surgery and it has been a journey during that time. It has been like a roller coaster ride. The highs with the breast casting and the overwhelming love and support extended to JaMichael and my mother by family and friends, to the low of having a "coded." But, just like a ride, I was on top with flowers being delivered and friends visiting me at the hospital and at home—to the drop, with an issue with one of my drains. I've wanted to reach back out to the many people who have called, but being on the phone is a task, as my breathing still has to improve. As the days go on, I pray that I continue to enjoy the ride to the top and the unexpected encounters are ones that continue to build on the breast cancer mantra of faith and hope. This ride requires you to be filled with both before you get on, and if for some reason you don't have both, surrounding yourself with people who will stand in the gap on your behalf.

Unconditional love

May 31, 2013 11:02 p.m.

I honestly have found strength in the love and prayers of many of you reading this, but also because of my mother, who as a single mother, had to exemplify strength. Not to mention, my husband who after taking his vows less than a year ago, was given the opportunity to bow out but has stood by my side. Since the surgery, I have realized the full motion of our arms that we often take for granted, as I only have pain, for now, in most motions. I have come to realize the simple things aren't so simple when you don't have the basic physical capability, such as getting in the bed, wiping after using the rest room. . .I know, TMI. . .lol, bathing, squeezing a stress ball, and lifting your arms just to get dressed. All seems simple until you can't. *Simple until you can't,* and then you don't know how long you can't, and when you can at what capacity.

But unconditional love comes in when you shower for the first time and can't dry yourself, and your husband steps in because he doesn't want you to be frustrated or feel sorry for yourself. He not only made sure I was dry, but applied the lotion and had me smelling good. That love is exemplified by setting an alarm clock to give me medicine at 3 a.m. and then having to be up to go to work at 5 a.m. That has been JaMichael's life the past week. But that one moment when you know you are loved unconditionally is when you require assistance after using the bathroom and without hesitation, someone comes to wipe you and tells you that should never be ashamed or embarrassed, and then makes sure you really feel comfortable by getting you your favorite cupcake ☺ My sorority's chaplain discussed this during her visit in the hospital with me. She discussed the love she felt when speaking with JaMichael and how it reminded her of the love Christ had for the church, Corinthians 13:1. It is love that bears all things. This is the love that made me fight when I coded after surgery. This is the love that I always dreamed about but never thought I would experience. This love is the one that gives me strength when I don't have energy because I know there is much more work for me to do.

I've seen that unconditional love in my mother, as she became a rock for JaMichael during a period of uncertainty at the hospital. She has semi-moved into assist, and despite her physical limitations, she makes sure I am okay first. Through this entire journey, other than the initial diagnosis of cancer I had not seen her cry until today. They removed two drains and the pain was unbearable, and so while I tried to be as strong as I could with the least amount of emotion, I had to cry, and I looked over and she was wiping her eyes. My Soror said that a mother never anticipates that they will be the ones visiting their children in the hospital for things such as this, and when they do it takes a lot out of them. So, sometime over this weekend, I will finally cry because, in her own unspoken words, my mother said it was okay.

Recovery

Oct 8, 2013 7:09 p.m.

It has been awhile, and the recovery journey was and has been truly a journey. It has made me recognize what all life has to offer and what LIVING really is. In order to LIVE I had to de-clutter, and I will say that is a process in itself. I was able to attend my sorority's Centennial Celebration in Washington, DC, and spend time with a one of my closest girlfriends from Detroit and my Sands. I then found the strength to make it to Project LEAD in San Diego, CA, a week later. It was trying on my body and mental psyche once I felt my body being strained, but the science behind cancer; a must for me.

I met some wonderful women in the program and learned that there is so much work to be done in the cancer realm. I know I don't want my younger cousins and *definitely* not my two goddaughters to ever experience breast cancer, so my responsibility to them is to advocate now for more research, encourage people to be a part of clinical trials, but most importantly be at the table when decisions around the disease are being made. While I was in San Diego, my one-year wedding anniversary came and went, and while it was hard for me to not be with JaMichael, I felt like I had purpose for being there and I knew we would be celebrating the following week. And we did just that in Cancun, with the Isoms, which made it truly memorable. While I did more than I probably should have, I did my physical therapy daily, prayed for strength, and continue to pray for my spirit to be restored. Recovery of the soul and the spirit has probably been the hardest and most unexpected. I haven't fully recovered but know that I will.

One Year

Dec 14, 2013 9:09 p.m.

I have mixed emotions, but today, December 14, marks one year since I got my cancer diagnosis. It's kind of like remembering what I was doing on 9/11/2001 when the planes hit the twin towers. December 14, 2012. . .I was at home recovering from a myomectomy and watching the Newtown school shooting unfold on TV, and thinking to myself how I was going to have to protect my little one as much as possible and counting down the days until we could start trying again. Then I got THE call. I was home alone because I wanted JaMichael to get some time for himself, and it was the Christmas season.

I wanted to call my Granny because she would know what to do but she left us on this side of heaven August 16, 2010. I was so confused and a part of me didn't want to tell anyone, but then the Spirit spoke to me and I called JaMichael and then my mother; the two people that love me the most. In hindsight, I maybe should have planned that a bit better because they both reacted in a way that you only see in the movies and in a way that you would never want to inflict on the ones you love. So, here I am a year later...five surgeries later...cancer free. But it has been a truly long and emotional journey. People that I would have never thought cared or would go above and beyond, and who hadn't known me for that long stepped up (my Leadership Buckhead crew), I became extremely close to some special ladies, I connected with some phenomenal women in my new sisterhood, my family showed up not only for me but for my mother, and my friends...AMAZING...while some were lost along the way, my friends loved and supported me even when I didn't do it for myself. So, today my emotions are mixed because I'm reflecting on the decisions I made, the brave women on the journey that didn't make it this year, living life to the fullest. I'm also thinking about what my future has in store and whether my dreams are just deferred or if they are not going to ever be a reality. I wanted to celebrate but opted to lie low today and just do church. My soul was filled when the subject was shared. . ."It Doesn't Add Up" and the Scripture was James 1:2-4. Once I heard the Word, I knew that today was my day, and the day I want to celebrate with my friends and family is the day I became cancer free, May 21, 2013. This is the time that it got real for my friends and family, and so I want to celebrate THRIVING with them on that day. Today was my day to know that through the trials comes joy.

So here I am today, bolder, stronger, and THRIVING. I have now been cancer free for two years, and am abundantly blessed for that. The two years haven't been without a few extra bumps along the way; a biopsy and two additional surgeries. In the end, I know that God continues to smile on me and bring me through it all. I have continued to meet fabulous women of all ages and developed meaningful relationships with them. Each woman I meet feeds my soul and assists God in helping me get to my destiny. The journey has been a powerful one, but it has given me so much despite the peaks and valleys. I have grown in ways I would have never imagined. I have a different appreciation and outlook on life. I recognized there have been times through this journey where the Lord carried me because it was too overwhelming for me; but He never left me. So for that reason alone, I must continue to be the voice for those too afraid, the face of those too ashamed, and the hope that many have lost. Through my eyes there is much more work to be done along my journey.

Lisa Ford

Age: 48

Tennessee

One-Year Survivor/Thriver

ABOUT THE AUTHOR

Lisa Ford is the proud mother of two beautiful children, Kara Faith, 20, and Chase, 15. She is also so proud that she is the sixth child (four sisters and one brother) of awesome parents. Lisa has been employed with SunTrust Bank for 29 years and loves her job. She is a very competitive sports enthusiast who loves all sports and activities, such as bowling and playing corn hole (or bean bag toss).

CHAPTER FOUR

LEARNING TO THRIVE WHEN SURVIVING CANCER

by Lisa Ford

I remember the day in March, 2013, after having a mammogram come back odd-looking, going to have more pictures taken of my left breast. This was not anything unusual, as every time I had a mammogram I was called back for more pictures because my breasts were so dense. This time I actually was called in with the doctor that read the results. She told me there was an area of concern and that she wanted me to have a biopsy, especially with our family history.

I remember going in to have the biopsy of my breast. I had never quite experienced anything like this, and I felt like they were just being on the safe side by taking a biopsy with our family history. One of my elder sister's (Betty) was also diagnosed with breast cancer approximately 18 years ago. She had one breast removed and the doctor's told her the cancer was not in her lymph nodes, therefore there was no need for chemo. The next year…the cancer was back and all in her bones. It ended up moving to her brain and killing her. She was only 38 years old when she died. It was a horrific experience to watch someone you love go through this and see what the cancer can do to a person. Therefore, when I was given the news in the doctor's office the week after the biopsy that I did have cancer, I was filled with all kinds of emotions.

Thankfully, I had three very important people with me when I was given the news. I had my sister Terry, my sister Diane (who is a nurse), and my boyfriend Mike. I could not have had better support by my side throughout the entire process. I knew at that time that it was up to God to help me through this. See, I go to church every Sunday…but always yearned to have a closer relationship with the Lord…never sure how to get there or what to do. This was a big stepping stone for me. I still have a long way to go…but I definitely feel like I am on the right path. I never blamed God at all for anything. I thankfully had great parents that taught us that God was always there to help us, not hurt us. My mom was a true inspiration, as well, as she found out she had lung cancer and died one month from the day she found out. Never batted an eye…was ready to see the Lord, even though she was in her early 70s. I learned a tremendous amount from her and my dad who suffered with bladder cancer in his 40s. They removed his bladder and he is now 85. With all of the cancer that our family has experienced—you can see why it was so terrifying when I got the news.

When the doctor told me that I definitely had breast cancer…I was determined to be strong. I did well until I looked over and saw the look on my sister's face—of terror, and she was about to let loose on the tears. When she started crying, I started crying—we all started crying. It's hard not to cry when everyone around you is crying. My boyfriend Mike was crying harder than anyone…the doctor even said that he might be the one that needed medication. I cannot begin to tell you how important it is to have that support. I had to get control of myself and my emotions. All I could think about when I found out is, how was I going to tell my children, who were 17 (Kara) and 12 (Chase) at the time. They knew about my sister's dying and the word cancer terrified them. My son had texted me as soon as we had walked out of the doctor's office asking if I had cancer. I did not want to tell him over a text that I did. I also didn't want to lie about it. I went home that day and when they walked in from school I told them that I had been diagnosed with breast cancer. I told them that we thought that we had caught it very early, but that I was having a test in the next day or two which would show everything.

I was very positive. I told them I was scared, but that I knew that with their help I could get through it. I was divorced, and my children lived with me since going through the divorce approximately three years prior. There was a lot of tension between my daughter, Kara, and me, as she did not like the guy that was so beneficial in getting me through this time of my life, Mike. Unfortunately, she seemed very bitter throughout my entire process, as he was by my side through it all and she was not happy about that. It did add a lot of stress for me as I love them both. My goal through this was to keep the kids far enough away that they would only see the positive....no negative...no crying! I needed the adults to lean on as I had plenty of breakdown times and plenty of crying!

The day came for me to have the MRI with IV contrast to get a better picture of exactly how much cancer we were looking at. I was told that I could have something to relax me before the MRI, but because of my being hard-headed, I said that I would be completely fine. After arriving and getting the IV they rolled me into the MRI, and I felt like I couldn't breathe! I could only imagine what the people were going to see as this big machine started taking pictures. I almost yelled to stop the test as I was so anxious...I thought I was hyperventilating. I finally started praying to God to give me the strength to get through the test. I wanted to know what I was looking at.

He did...He helped me get through the MRI. I have never felt the way I felt in that room....very scared, but after I prayed about it...it was weird how I calmed down enough to get through the test. To say the least, after walking back into the waiting room where my sister, Diane, and Mike were waiting I was just exhausted with worry about what the technicians that did the test could see. I was trying to be so strong, but my sister could see right through me.   Before I got in the car, she said Lisa...Are you okay? I burst into tears. I think it was just the nerves and the not knowing—just the stress. I felt like a wreck! This would be the first of many times that I broke down. She could tell that I was upset and I was trying to hold everything inside. She told me to let it out! I did that day!

After about a week I had an appointment with the breast surgeon to get the results of the MRI. I was nervous, but knew that I had no control, so my goal was to give my anxious worries to God and let Him help me through whatever news we did get. I did the best I could with that! At this appointment I found out that I had Stage 1 cancer in my left breast. This was good news. I didn't even have to think about the plan of action. The nurse started giving me options and I told her I wanted the complete mastectomy. The last thing I wanted to do is go through this whole process and a year or two later get the cancer on the other side. I took that option away.

We scheduled the double mastectomy and I felt like I was as calm as a person could be. We scheduled the surgery for early April, 2012. I had never been in the hospital for anything "big," besides having my two children. This was definitely traumatic for me. I had my sisters, Terry and Diane, my boyfriend, Mike, and my dad with me when we were given the results that I had Stage 1. We were all relieved to a certain extent, and there was no crying…only smiles at this appointment. I was a wreck at night when I tried to sleep—wondering how I was going to get through this and take care of my children. I knew, where there is a will there is a way!

The next step was scheduling an appointment with an oncologist. My sister, Diane, took me to the appointment. When the doctor started talking about a year of chemo and losing my hair, eyelashes, etc. I couldn't stop crying. She discussed everything with the doctor…I cried the entire appointment. I have no idea really what was discussed. She knew the medical terms and she understood it…I had no idea, so I just continued to cry while she talked with the doctor. We scheduled the chemo to begin after I healed from the double mastectomy that I would be having in a couple of weeks.   Diane always told me to let it out, and on this day I *definitely* let it out. I couldn't stop crying.

The day of the surgery I was very strong until they called my name in the waiting room to get ready for the surgery. I hugged my boyfriend Mike, who was there by my side, and my sister, Diane. I cried walking to the nurse and didn't quit crying until they knocked me out for the surgery. Not sure why it hit me at that time, but it did. I think sometimes we try to be strong for everyone else…when we need to just let go and know that we will get the support and help from God that we need to get through it. My children did not understand why I was so insistent that they not come to the hospital the day of the surgery. The fact of the matter is, I didn't want them to see me fall apart!

They were angry with me but I knew that I was going to fall apart at some point, and I just thought it would be best for them to see me after the surgery. I just thought it was better to have my sisters, my boyfriend and my dad there for support for me and didn't want to traumatize the kids. The surgery was late in the afternoon, so I didn't get into my room until, like, 8 p.m. I was out of it. I do not remember much of the time I spent in the hospital. I think they kept me sedated pretty well. My children came up and visited, but in all honesty…I just do not remember much. My main goal was to stay positive and smile as much as I could around the kids.

I am so thankful to have a sister that is a nurse (Diane), and if there were ever any questions about anything she was on top of it. Once getting home, my sister bathed me and changed the bandages, and my boyfriend was always there to help and took care of the wonderful "grenades" (drains) that had to be measured three times a day. I had two drains on each side of my body. When I looked in the mirror the first time after the surgery I literally got sick to my stomach. It was not a pretty sight at all. I had the expanders put in so that I could have reconstruction later after my treatments. The incisions across my chest and under my arms were major.

I never imagined getting through this. It was such a traumatic thing to go through and to know that I was facing a year of chemo after I recovered from this just added to it. Thankfully, with the help of my support system, friends, neighbors and my children I recovered from the mastectomy.

The next step in the process was getting a port put in for the chemo treatments. This was just an outpatient procedure, and was not bad at all. I had an incision right above my right expander. This was a breeze compared to the double mastectomy. . . . It did not really faze me at all. The next week I was starting chemo, so I was very nervous about it. I tried to always stay very positive about it all. I think half of the battle is staying positive and focusing on getting better. I am the type of person that has a reaction to everything, so I was definitely concerned about the treatments and just everything in general. My main concern throughout everything was not the loss of my breasts, but the loss of my hair. This was the most traumatic thing about going through the entire process to me. I do have to say though that my sisters Terry and Diane went with me to buy wigs. I think they had more fun trying on different wigs than I did…they definitely made something that is not typically fun to do fun!

We had everyone in the store laughing at us. That is typically what happens when we are all together!

The first chemo treatment was in May of 2012. I was very nervous. I tried, as always, to be the strong person that I wanted to be, but when I was alone…was so far from that! I always had my sister, Diane, or my boyfriend Mike with me at all chemo treatments. Most treatments Diane would take me, and Mike would come up on his lunchtime and sit with me. My daughter actually came to a couple as well. Again…the support was there. I remember when I went in the very first time and picked a chair to sit in there was a really young girl sitting next to me. She was having her last treatment but had a really hard time….she had so much anxiety when getting the treatments. I felt so bad for her…and wondered if I would be the same way every week. After hearing all of the dos and don'ts after a treatment, I made it through the first treatment that lasted almost the entire day.

I made it through without any hiccups, and, once home, within about three hours started with the dry heaves. I felt very sick to my stomach and kept a bucket right next to me on the sofa. My sisters always came to visit and make sure I was taken care of. I know it was hard on the kids coming home from school and seeing me sick. Even though I felt like death, my goal was to stay positive and show my kids that I was going to get through this. My daughter did not offer to help when my boyfriend Mike was there, as she was very angry that he was there. She just didn't realize everything that he did for me. She still, to this day, has no idea. As she matures, one day she will realize that he was put into my life for a reason. And even though she didn't like the thought of me giving my attention to someone other than her 24-7, she will one day know that he was a good part of my life.

The day after my treatments (the first four the strongest), I had to go and get a shot in my stomach to help keep my resistance up as much as possible. The shot was nothing…but I would typically get a bag of fluids as well to help with the nausea. My sister would give me a bag of fluids as well, at times, when I was very sick to my stomach. The first four treatments were the worst. I had a treatment every other week. I cut my hair off really short and as soon as it started really coming out, after my second treatment, I had my hair dresser come to the house and shave it off. I just sat and cried. I have always had a thick head full of red hair. I did cut it and donate it to Locks of Love so that some child would have some pretty red hair and feel really good about the way he or she looks, even with a wig on!

I remember the day after getting my head shaved and feeling so ugly, Mike coming into the house and kissing me on the cheek and telling me I was beautiful. He was so loving and positive throughout the entire process. He was very affectionate and loving…even when I felt I looked like an alien. I honestly think without him I would not have made it through. I had the love and help of my sisters and children…but there was a different love that he showed…inexplicable. I will never, ever forget it. I do believe God puts people in your life for a reason.

After the first four treatments I started having treatments weekly. I went back to work after my second treatment with my wig on. It was tough, but the love I felt from the people I work with was amazing as well. I would typically miss the day of chemo, and while going through the first four I missed a few days after each treatment. Once I started going weekly, they did not affect me that much. I missed the day I had the treatment, and would return to work the next day. My stomach was not upset. I was more exhausted and just didn't have much energy at this point. After several months of these treatments I went to an even lighter dose, which was every three weeks. I continued the chemo for a full year. I never had to miss a treatment because my levels were off. I was amazed, but so very thankful as I was ready to get my hair back and have my reconstruction surgery. God was beside me the entire time!

The reconstruction process is a big process in itself. When they removed my breasts they put in those expanders that I mentioned earlier, which would be filled to stretch my skin so that I could eventually have an implant, which would make me look like a normal person again. The expanders were not the most comfortable things, but the process was not bad, and it was well worth it. I am thrilled with the way my implants look and, fortunately, I was able to keep my nipples, so you would not even really be able to tell I had been through this whole process....unless you looked really close at all the scars! I am very much glad I went through the reconstruction process!

In the midst of my treatments, I had a hard time keeping up with the home that my children and I lived in for the past 11 years. I could not do the yard work by myself (although I did), and the house needed a new heat/air unit, roof, all new appliances, etc. I could not afford to deal with it all. I decided to put my house on the market and was hoping I would be through my treatments before having to move. To say the least, I sold the house in about three days. I am not sure it was a good idea, as I was stressed packing a home that had been lived in for 11 years. I got rid of all of my furniture, as I wanted to start fresh.

This was very hard for me, as it did not sit well with my children, but financially I knew I didn't have a choice. I knew the kids would have to move in with their dad as I moved in with my sister, Diane, who had pretty much taken me to each chemo treatment, and who was with me at the doctor's appointments. She had a small apartment in lower level of her home. It was pretty devastating to me when I moved in with her, as my children moved in with their dad. The apartment was really nice...but I was very depressed, as I felt like I had lost everything, my home, my children, etc. I cried a lot...but with God's help I pulled myself out of the depression and pushed forward.

My son came and stayed with me on the days he was supposed to, which was nice. I am sure he was not thrilled about coming to stay in this tiny apartment with me, but I think he did enjoy his cousin and the farm that we were on. We fed the cows and just really had some good times there. He was very loving toward me during this time and is very thoughtful. I will always be grateful to my sister and her family for having me at their home for a year.

I finished my treatments while living with Diane and her family and had my reconstruction surgery as well. Everything went well. In September of 2014 I moved into a condominium, and I am really enjoying it. I could not have made it through this entire process without my family, children, friends and my boyfriend at the time. I do believe that everything happens for a reason, and people are brought into your life for a reason. A support system is a *must* through this process. My goal at this point is to help as many people going through this process as possible. I am working on starting a breast cancer group for women/men at church and hoping that it will be helpful. I am continuing to work on my relationship with God and know that with Him in my life…there is nothing I need to be afraid of. This is my story! ☺

I want to thank people that were so supportive in my life throughout this process: my children, Kara and Chase; my sisters, Terry and Diane; my boyfriend at the time, Mike; my dad, David; my neighbor, Jean; my girlfriends Terri and Tina, and all the random people that prayed for me and didn't even know me. Also, I include my brother, David, who had his church praying for me. Prayer is the answer!

My only advice to anyone going through this is to have a supportive group pf people who will be there for you when you need them. God helped me through this process and will help you through it as well! Keep your faith and always believe that you are never alone in any situation. Proud to be a survivor!

Mandy Ann Fridge

Age: 65

Georgia

Three-Year Survivor/Thriver

ABOUT THE AUTHOR

Born in Kansas City, MO, Mandy recently retired from AT&T after 45 years of service. She is actively involved with the AT&T Pioneers. This is a network of volunteers who effect immediate, tangible change in our local communities.

Mandy is also involved in several ministries at her church. She has three children and seven grandchildren, and currently resides in Atlanta, GA.

CHAPTER FIVE

FOURTH STRIKE

by Mandy Ann Fridge

The old saying of three strikes and you are out comes to mind when I think back to when this cancer journey began. In my case, it was four strikes before the ugly cancer creature attacked my right breast.

Why "four strikes"? I have had three biopsies over the past several years because of lumps that I found during my self-exams (an important monthly ritual). Three of them were benign. However, when I went to have my annual mammogram on my birthday, April 2, 2011, little did I know that this one was going to be, as Fred Sanford, would say "the **BIG** one!!?"

The technician at Emory Hospital Mammography Center and I carried on a jovial conversation and she complimented me on my appearance as looking like a 45-year-old rather than a 62-year-old (even with the grey hair that I have had since the age of 19)! Being myself, I had to take a bow and do a "twirl"…not knowing that the bad news hammers were yet to come.

I went about my day feeling good that I had gotten the mammogram done for the year. It's a curious thing that we don't know what the next day, week, month or year will bring. Within two weeks, I received the call that I needed to have further testing. I did not take it that seriously because I wanted to believe that it was because of the fibroids that there was not a true reading. I guess it was my way of self-diagnosing and self-medicating.

However, all kinds of thoughts ran through my mind. I remembered that each Sunday I would pray that the Lord would give me strength and good health so that I would be able to continue to support my family during their hours of need.

My brother fell off a ladder and broke his arm. I helped him to get medical attention. My mother had been hospitalized for a week. I worked from the hospital to help my brother with her care. My son had surgery for a tumor in his neck. I was able to work from home three months to help him get back on his feet. I guess I figured that I was everyone's Florence Nightingale.

I did not want to tell any of my family, so I went through all the testing alone (biopsies, ultrasounds). I received the call at 6 p.m., as I sat in my car about to go home from work. What a bummer! Cancer!! I was advised that I had been assigned a surgeon, Dr. Toncred Styblo, and that I had an appointment on the following Monday. I don't really remember much about that weekend except that it was a long one!

I do remember doing a Google search on the doctor, who, it turned out, was very accomplished:

- *Associate Professor of Surgery, Department of Surgery, Emory University School of Medicine*
- *Surgical Director, Breast Center, Winship Cancer Institute of Emory University*
- *Co-Director, High Risk Assessment Clinic, Winship Cancer Institute*

Since 1996, Dr. Styblo has been consistently named one of America's Top Surgeons and been listed in Best Doctors in America. She has also received three Cancer Liaison Physician Outstanding Performance Awards from the American College of Surgeons Commission on Cancer. Since joining the Emory surgical faculty in 1988, she has been active both locally and nationally in clinical and translational research.

Now, this information made me feel a little bit more at ease! However, when she and I discussed my options, it became cloudy again.

My diagnosis was Invasive Ductal Carcinoma Grade (Stage One), at 9 o'clock on my right breast, with estrogen and progesterone receptors. Whoever knew that there were many types of breast cancer! Now the clouds started really moving in. She advised that I would share in the decision for my treatment. As I thought to myself, "You are the one that went to school for many years to become a doctor. Shouldn't you (Dr. Styblo) be making the call?" Surgery, chemo, radiation! We decided that I would have surgery and then radiation, since it was only Stage One.

It was at this point that I decided I needed to confide in my family. Everyone seemed to be taking it harder than me. I looked at it like it was the luck of the draw, and I pulled the short straw. My solace was with the knowledge that I had the Lord on my side. I came to the summation that the Lord was telling me to be still and let this pass.

My 91-year-old mother, my brother and my eldest son all went to the hospital with me: the same family members that I had nursed back to health previously.

The surgery went well and I came home that afternoon after I recovered. I had thought that I would be there at least two days (times have changed). Dr. Styblo advised that she had tested my lymph nodes immediately after surgery and did not find any cancer. However, samples would be sent to the pathologist in California, and we would not have results until two weeks. They found a minute amount of cancer in the samples of my lymph nodes. This bumped it up to Stage Two. Now I would have to take chemo, radiation and lymphedema therapy.

Lymphedema therapy was another new term for me. Lymph nodes filter fluid as it flows through them, trapping bacteria, viruses and other foreign substances, which are then destroyed by special white blood cells called lymphocytes. Without normal lymph drainage, fluid can build up in the affected arm or leg, and lymphedema can develop. I was a candidate for lymphedema because I had several nodes removed during my surgery. Here was another opportunity for me to get up extra early for four weeks of appointments. I had to drive to Northside Hospital for the therapy, which included massages of the arm and wearing compression sleeves for the four weeks, and possibly for life!

With my strong religious belief and the support of my family and all my friends, I was ready to tackle all of this head on. Within three and a half weeks I was back at work. This was another surprise to me; I thought at least six weeks! The doctor advised that she could not justify my being off any longer.

The chemo came first and I needed to have four sessions—one every three weeks. I decided that I would have the treatment on a Friday and also take Monday off from work. This allowed me three days to recuperate. There would be at least two members of my family or a friend who would go with me to support me and drive my car. I had heard horror stories of how patients would get terribly sick during chemo. However, this was one challenge that I did not have to face; it did not make me sick at all!

One of the side effects of chemo did get to me. My hair! I knew that I was supposed to lose it, but often humans think that they can be the exception to the rule. That would be me! I had read books on cancer that advised to cut it before it fell out. I remember that I was about to leave the house and was combing my hair. It came out in a handful. I stayed home and had my son shave it off. I have not looked back; I have worn my hair very short ever since.

Radiation was next—five days a week for six weeks. I had a standing appointment at 7:30 each morning so that I could go to work afterwards. The only challenge was that the radiation oncologist had to mark up my upper body with markers and tape. The challenge was not to wash it off. Mission accomplished!

This all took place within six months. As I look back now I feel that all of this was a sign to me that I should not be trying to do everything. I needed to back off of some of the things that I always felt that I had to be a part of. The world would continue to revolve whether I was directing or not.

I encourage anyone that is facing a cancer challenge to do their research and become educated about their particular type. Take the time to sit down with your family to discuss. And most importantly, "Let go and let God"!

Merica Ann Griffin

Age: 68
Georgia

Two-Year
Survivor/Thriver

ABOUT THE AUTHOR

Merica Ann Griffin is an entrepreneur who has made her alteration and couture business into a great success over the 30 years she has been established in Atlanta, GA.

A "Grady baby," she was born in "the ATL" and attended Atlanta Public Schools, a fact of which she is very proud. After learning her seamstress skills in secondary school, Merica parlayed them into mastery through apprenticeships in alteration shops in the city's Sandy Springs and Buckhead communities. Over the years, she has had a range of interesting clients, including three Georgia governors and celebrity athletes from the world of Atlanta professional sports.

Merica is the mother of two grown sons, Quinn and Garrett, grandmother to six grandkids and great-grand to two. She is also a devoted 33-year congregant of Salem Bible Church and serves as a chorister in the choir and volunteers with several church ministries.

CHAPTER SIX

A TIME TO BE TESTED

by Merica Ann Griffin

I went to the doctor that day. It was actually, for something else—for knee pain. My blood pressure was also high, so while I was there they gave me a primary care physician to see, and a bunch of tests including a mammogram screening. They gave me a screening in August of 2012. That first mammogram came back and they saw something, so I had to have a second one.

It took about two screenings for the doctor to see what he needed to see. The test didn't show anything the first time. On the second one, the doctor said he wanted to schedule a biopsy and sonogram. The tissue was taken, and then that's when the tests revealed that I had Stage 1 breast cancer.

With cancer they treat your breast like a clock, and they said mine was at one o'clock in the left breast. My physician had a talk with me and explained what was going on. I felt like I was in a dream. I didn't really feel like I knew what was going on! But I knew I was in the hands of the best care possible. I was benefiting from the Winship Program of Emory University, which does cancer research, and which plays a role by going into Grady Hospital, since Grady is a training hospital. At the time, Winship was doing studies on women who had breast cancer but who did not have a family history of it, and my doctor was Dr. Sheryl Gabram.

What they said would happen was I would have to have an operation, and they didn't know whether or not it would be a total mastectomy. My cancer was estrogen-based and it was spiraling outward. They asked me so many questions! Like, about my sex life—I had to fill out *a lot* of questionnaires. They wanted to know how I would feel if I had to lose one breast. Was I sexually active? Would I get depressed? I told the lady, "No, I am not sexually active. My main concern is if you can get this cancer out of me! Sex...now, that is not what I'm going to be worried about! Do I *look* like I'm sexually active at age 65??" The clinician said, Ms. Griffin, "Now, how do you feel about this?" And I said, "It is what it is!" That clinic worker said, "Aren't you going to be depressed?" and I said, "No, I know who the Ultimate Healer is."

When I told my children, Quinn didn't take it so well. He doesn't take illness well, but he tried to be strong for me. Garrett was a little different. He didn't have a problem with it—"How can I help you, Mom?" is all he said. My brothers and sisters were just fabulous. Amazing! My youngest brother, Ben, moved me into my new apartment; he actually lived there and cooked for me.

My church was very supportive. There was *always* somebody checking on me, sending me cards and words of inspiration. They sent money, made sure I knew what was going on and what was on the church calendar. They prayed for me. My family was there for sure—and even my customers! They brought me meals; gave me gifts of money and even donated some pretty **big gifts** like a new living room suite, which I really needed at the time for my new apartment. People would come over and take Ben, my brother, to the store for me, since also at the time neither of us had any dependable transportation

But it was my eldest sister, Linda, who *really* was my caregiver. Linda did most of it. She took care of me after the surgery coming home from the hospital. And my Aunt Lee was at the surgery all day long! When they did the partial mastectomy and lumpectomy, I opted to have the reconstruction surgery at the same (the procedure is called a "Free flap"). They told me I would be in there for eight hours, but I was actually in there for 16. Lee and Linda stayed there the entire time.

When I went in for surgery that morning, and when I opened my eyes up in the Recovery area, the first thing I demanded was, "Is that clock the right time?" "Geez, we haven't *ever* seen anybody who woke up like *that* before!" the nurses all said. "Well, you know, all the clocks at Grady aren't always set at the right time," I explained, really.... not believing it could actually *be* that time. I couldn't believe that I'd been under *that long*.

I didn't want an implant, but after my friend Myrtice and I did some research I had decided on the reconstruction, which was done by Dr.

Angela Cheng. My oncologist could not believe how beautiful it was! I said, "Yeah, but it's so big! It's about as big as a grapefruit; and a little bigger than the other one." But *everything that is in the breast is mine*—they took the fatty tissue from my stomach and part of the muscle. This was a new procedure. In this procedure they checked the front part of me, and then they checked the back. "You can take as much fat from my stomach as you want to," I said. "I got too much anyway."

Two plastic surgeons did the work; kind of like you do a C-section where they made an incision, pulled out the fat, put in some mesh. . . . Afterwards, they would come into the Recovery room every hour saying, "It's *alive!*" and checking my breast to make sure the area was doing fine, and to see how my body was taking all of this.

I applaud the people at Grady and Emory. They took *very* good care of me. Even months after the surgery they watched to make sure I wasn't getting any unwanted swelling anywhere else. I was blessed all the way around.

I've talked to women, and have learned how fortunate I was to have caught it as quickly as we did. I was not showing any signs of cancer. I'm so vigilant now. I had been stressed out about what was I was going through in my life at the time—and by being an entrepreneur and self-employed, it often was so hard to keep up with the cost of health insurance.

When I went out on my own I tried to keep it, and then I would lose it. I would just pray, "God, I don't have health insurance." So I would ask *Him* to help me. I would just eat well, look after myself well, and I was walking at the time. . . When I found out I had cancer, Medicare had just kicked in for me. I got Medicare at the first of the year, and then I was officially diagnosed in November of 2012! April of 2013 is when I had the surgery.

#1, I had the BEST team of doctors—and they were all women, and so were all of the techs. They were *so good* at what they do. My family and my Church were all taking care of me. I kept a positive mind, and I put God in everything. Right before I had the anesthesia, one of the nurses gently held my hand and prayed with me. I just thank God that this experience, overall, wasn't as severe as it could have been.

In an effort to keep an open mind about this whole process, I go to support meetings when I can. I also attend nutrition classes to educate myself on the benefits to myself and others. When other people in the group tell their stories I feel so blessed that my journey was not as difficult as some. You see, I endured a small portion of what they went through, all the more reason to thank God for the doctors and technicians at Grady Hospital (my birthplace) for their thorough work.

I would like to become an advocate for early detection and mammogram testing to get the word out to those who don't know how important this is. Now that I'm retired, I have more time to devote to volunteering at my church, as well as spending time with my grandchildren and family.

What I can say and know for sure is…. that this was a time in life when, truly, my strength, resilience, and faith were all tested.

Katrina Hayes

Age: 47

North Carolina

16-Year Survivor/Thriver

ABOUT THE AUTHOR

Katrina is a born-and-raised North Carolinian. She is one of seven children and has one daughter who is a graduate of Florida State University. Katrina is currently in the process of writing her own personal novel about how her faith in God has helped her overcome the trials and obstacles she has faced from her "WIN" over breast cancer.

CHAPTER SEVEN

LET GO AND LET GOD

by Katrina Hayes

My journey of breast cancer all began when I found the lump on my breast myself—and how it has changed my life forever!

I will never forget the moment of discovery. I was lying on my couch one Sunday and felt something on my breast that was not there before. I went to the bathroom to see what it was, and it was a knot. The next day I called the doctor so I could go and see what was going on with my left breast. When I went to the doctor, she asked me all kinds of questions about my family history and did cancer run in my family, and I said no. Then she said that I would need to go and see a specialist so that they could take a closer look to see what was going on.

The nurse made me an appointment and said they would call when it was scheduled. Not long after that, I got the call to go and see the specialist in Wilmington. My doctor was at that time Dr. Tinsley. When he came in the room after seeing my x-rays, he said I would need to have a biopsy done so they could find out what the knot was. A nurse made me an appointment for June 7th, 1999, and it was done in Outpatient. The doctor said once they got the results back he would call and talk to me about what they had found. I went home and rested up after the minor surgery. It was about two weeks after that when the nurse called and told me they had gotten my results back and needed me to come so I could talk to the doctor about what he had found.

It was nerve-racking to know I was on my way to see the doctor to discuss what was wrong with my breast. So it was time, and before I knew it, I was on my way to Wilmington to go and see the doctor. The closer we got, the more my stomach was in knots. I got to the office, signed in, and they said we will call you back in a few minutes. I was just sitting in the doctor's office waiting for my name to be called and it seemed like they were *never* going to get to me. Then I heard my name, and my stomach just sank to the bottom, and the knots in my stomach really got tighter then!

The doctor came in and said they'd gotten my results back, and what they'd found was cancer: "You have breast cancer." I never thought I'd have received such shocking news that would change my life and body forever. When he said you have cancer I laughed to keep from crying. This was so hard and tough and *very rough* for me to hear. I did not expect to receive such shocking news that would change my life and body forever.

At that very moment, everything was still and I just went numb. The doctor started to talk about having surgery and that I needed to make a decision quickly.

I was thinking that I just got news that had turned my life upside down, and I needed to try and get myself together. On the inside I felt like broken pieces, and my heart was shattered. I still could not accept that this was me, but it *was,* and I had to be strong. When I finally got myself somewhat together, then I called the nurse to have the operation scheduled. It would be July 12th at 7 a.m. When I hung up the phone from the nurse I cried. This was getting ready to happen, and my breast was getting ready to be taken off, and my body was never being the same again. I prayed through the whole process, and this was what really got me through it all. I had other people praying for me, also, when it was time for me to go to the hospital. I had my family, pastor, and church family to pray for me—and prayer works!

The day of the surgery the doctor came in and explained everything about the surgery and that he would not know how bad it was until he went in. I had another doctor that was going to operate on me also, and his name was Dr. Kay. He also talked to me and said he could tell that I had strong faith; he said that he knew that God would be guiding his hands through the operation and that everything will be just fine. When the surgery was over, the doctor came out and told my family everything went fine and that I was on my way to the recovery room. When I was coming around from the surgery, I was in so much pain! I had tubes in my arm and my stomach. One night, when my family left from visiting me and I was in my room all alone, I said to God that I can't do this by myself and I need Your help. Then, at the foot of my bed I saw an image of God; it was a white figure, and his arms stretched out and a bright light came from him.

I will never forget my personal experience with my Heavenly Father. One day the nurse came in to change my bed and she helped me into a wheelchair. While I was sitting there, tears began to roll down my face, and I cried like a baby. Reality hit me all at once that my breast was gone. I felt like I could not stop crying, the tears kept coming and coming like a nonstop river. The pain of it all, and to know that just hours before, nothing about me was different—but, now there was! There came a time while I was in the hospital when my legs went numb, and I didn't know why. A nurse came in my room and she looked at me and said, "We are going to get you through this; God won't put any more on you than you can bear." They wrapped my legs up in stockings so that the circulation would come back in my legs, and it was two days later that my legs got better.

I spent a week in the hospital, and the doctor came and told me I was going to be released July 18. I was thinking to myself, it's time to go home as a different person. I knew that through all of this that I was leaning and depending on God like never before. He brought me though the surgery, and He was going to take me through the rest of the healing process. I knew that my life was not going to be the same and that I was somehow going to be a better person because of it. There are *so many* stages you go through with having breast cancer, and you need support from your family. This was a time in my life when I was scared; and I would be *lying* if I said that I wasn't afraid. But, that is when my faith met fear head on! I was not going to let this beat me I had too much to live for and to do. My life was by no means over, and this was just a stepping stone I had to jump over to get to the *next chapter* of my life. I knew who I was, and who I belong to going through breast cancer. I was a child of the King. I knew I was a winner in Him, not in myself, but in God. I know that my Redeemer lives and he watches over me, no matter what I go through or comes my way.

While I was home, a nurse came to the house to check on my bandages and to check the tubes in my arm and stomach. She asked me one day was I in pain, and I said no, and she said to me, "God is good to you." I just smiled and said, yes He is good. When she would change my bandages, she would tell me how good my scars looked. I could not see, as I was lying down. As I was home still recovering from the surgery, my mind was working on how my body was going to look and the change that came along with the new me. I had to wear a binder around my stomach: that was where the doctor took fat from my stomach to make a breast.

It was drawing near the time for me to go back to the doctor so that he could take out the last tube in my arm and take off the bandages. When I walked into the doctor's office and they called my name, I got butterflies and I was heading back to see Dr. Tinsley; he said everything looked good. I was glad to hear that, but I still had to see my daughter, Elise, and my niece Lashonda. They took me home and, as we were on our way, reality hit in and *this* was it! The closer we got to home, the more I kept on saying "Hold me Jesus, just hold me." When we got home, I went in the bathroom and changed my clothes, and my eyes were closed in front of the mirror, and those same words I just kept on saying over and over again. I could not say anything else.

I started to cry as I began to turn around and face the mirror for the first time since the surgery. I saw my breast, and tears begin to come down my cheeks as I stared at my breast and how it had changed. *It was no longer what I was used to seeing every morning and night when I went to bed.* I took a deep breath and said, "It looks good." I knew at that very moment that I was going to be alright; how could I not be when Jesus had been holding me the whole time? I had to go and see the doctor a little while longer. Dr. Tinsley he said that he got it all, and that under my arm I had one bad lymph node that he had removed. Then it was time for the next stage of having breast cancer—and that was taking chemotherapy.

The nurse set me up an appointment to see an oncologist. The day when I went to see her, she explained everything about what was going to happen. Dr. Arb told me that, first, I needed to take some tests to make sure everything was alright for me taking the chemo. I had to take a heart test, and a bone test, and the entire round of tests came back good! I had to get a port-a-cath put in my chest. One problem was that my veins were too small.

I had surgery again on September 29, 1999, in the outpatient hospital. When I was on my way to the Recovery Room, and I was waking up from the medicine, the nurse gave me juice and crackers and I got sick and threw up and had to sit there a while until I felt better. I started taking the chemotherapy on October 7, 1999, and when the treatments began the side effects were awful. I got sick and felt weak and could not work. One day at my treatments I met a lady and her name was Linda. She was crying and she asked the nurse what my name was, and she told her it was Katrina. The woman wanted to know why I was not crying, and I told her that God was with me. She told me she was upset about losing her hair, and I said I was, too, and then she said that she had already brought her wig. We were two strangers that just met and were going through the same thing. It was good for us to talk to each other. We helped each other at that very moment; even though we both were going to lose our hair, it would grow back after the chemotherapy was complete.

I never knew so many people had breast cancer until I had to go through this myself. There were also *men* who had to take chemotherapy while I was taking mine!

In January of 2000, my blood count was low, and I could not take my treatments until it went back up. I had to take shots to get my hemoglobin back up so I could start again. I was getting an additional exam, and then found out that I had thyroid problems. So, I went to Dr. Arb for chemotherapy, and she found *more stuff to be wrong with me!* It's good that she found it all, and I got help for it while I was taking the chemotherapy. The next time I went back, on Friday 3rd of 2000, I started my next treatment. This was different; it was called Taxol. I had bad side effects: my hands and feet would start to burn, and I also got a numb feeling in them also. This treatment made me so sick! I got a terrible pain in my stomach while I was sitting in the chair, and the nurse had to go and get the doctor. They gave me some medicine to take, so the pain just stopped after a few minutes.

I met another woman while I was taking my treatments, and we began to talk. She began telling me how God was helping her get through the chemotherapy and that He never promised we would not have bad days. But we agreed -- God would see us through them all. As we kept on talking, she said that her view of sickness was different now. She said that she had more compassion for people than she did before. And I said I agreed with her.

It was time for me to another treatment of the Taxol; I did not get sick like I had before, but it did made me sleepy. When I returned home I took a nap, but when I woke up I began to feel the side effects of the medicine, and my whole body was aching all over. It later went away, and I felt a little better. It was time for me to go back and, this time, when I did, my hemoglobin was too low to take my treatment. So, the doctor said that I would need to take shots to bring it back up. I ended up taking 10 shots (all in my legs)! While I was waiting to go back to the doctor, I got a call from the nurse that my potassium was low. So, I needed to take more medicine to bring that back up while waiting on my blood pressure to get back to normal in order to finish taking the rest of my treatments.

FINALLY, my body got back to where I could take my treatments; I was ready because I was nearing the end of the chemotherapy. On May the 19th of 2000, I took my last treatment of chemotherapy, and I was so happy that it was over and done that I had finished all of my treatments, and that I had made it through it all with the help of God on my side. There were a lot of people along with me, taking chemotherapy. I had no idea the number of people that had cancer until it had happened to me. You just never really know until it hits home. While I was looking around the room, the spirits of these people were so high, and that made me feel so good to be in their company. At that time, I didn't want to be anywhere else but there, in the company of these brave and wonderful people!

I had to go and see the doctor once more so that my port-a-cath could be removed now that I had finished the chemotherapy. It went well, as with all of the surgeries I had to go through. I had to go back to Dr. Arb and she said that I would need to take some pills for five years. While I was recovering from this surgery, I had been thinking about all of the things that I had just been though and how my body was no longer the same. When I was going through, the enemy, which is the Devil, brought something to my mind, and one thought was, "Now that your body looks like that, who will ever love you that way? And I admit, for a moment He had me, and I began to cry and have a pity party just for that moment. But I shook myself and told that old Devil that he was a liar, and that God loves me and someone else will too! "Now take that, Devil, and get out of my head in the name of Jesus!"

I knew who I was and who was living on the inside of me, helping me get through it all. It was nobody but God. I had his Holy Spirit living on the inside of me, and when the Devil tried it—and he did—my faith just shut him down. I knew that what I had on the inside of me was greater than what was trying to come against me. I was more than a conquer, and I had won this battle with God by my side. Tell Him thank you, and that was what I did. But I still had to go through all of the changes that came with having breast cancer.

The biggest change I had to deal with, and adjust to, was the *new me*. And it was not easy at all when I looked in the mirror at my body I would still cry and have to tell myself you are still you, but just a bit different. I was not the same me, but a *better me* with more of me to love. I had just won another battle with God by my side and it felt good to knock that Devil down: he thought I was going to die, but I had too much to live for, and I knew that my journey needed to be told to help others that would walk in my same footsteps. I would need to let them know how God was with me giving me what I needed to make it through this cancer. He gave me his love, joy, peace, strength, courage, boldness and, but most of all, he gave me *Him* to hold onto in this very difficult time of my life.

When you know you are in the Master's hand, whatever you may be dealing with or going through at that time in your life, you will know that you can make it. I had to tell myself that a lot, and I knew that God was walking with me and talking to me and letting me know we are almost at the end of this battle and I am going to bring you out.

There is a song that rings in my Spirit when I think of how God has brought me through this cancer and it would be, " Lord I just want to thank you," And, yes, if I had a thousand tongues there would be no way to thank Him enough for all He has done for me during this cancer. I'm so glad that I know him and that my Redeemer lives. He just steps into your life when you need him the most, and lets you know that everything is going to be alright. He took me to His word and let me know that I will never leave you or forsake you. I am here with you, just as I was with Moses, so am I, too, with you through your cancer.

Something on the inside was working on the outside, and it brought a change to my life. It was God's Holy Spirit speaking to me and letting me know, fear not, I am here right by your side. It's so good to have people in your life or that you know who can get a prayer though while you are dealing with any kind of sickness. I'm so glad that I know the Lord and that He was the one that I needed the most while I was going through all of my cancer treatments, chemotherapy, sickness, and operations. This was not an easy fight. When I was weak, He was my strength, and when I was down His love lifted me, and when the pain would come, He was my comforter.

He had other plans for my life. I am so glad that he did. There are people that have *died* from breast cancer. My cousin had breast cancer and *she* died from it. That was just God's will for her life, and this was his will for my life: to tell my journey to help others out there. As I take a long look at it now, and how breast cancer came in my life, then how I was changed by it, I can say I would not change a thing about this journey. It has made me into a woman who wants to help many others that may be taking their journey right at this moment. When I know what it took for me to get through this, I want them to know and understand that the same God is with them that was and is with me. *God does not change. He stays the same today and forever more.*

When someone reads this personal journey of mine and the others, I want them to realize they are special in the sight of God, and that He loves them more than they will ever know. I am coming to end of my journey, and this is how I would like to end this chapter for all to read. Through all of the changes and pain that came with having breast cancer, it has brought me even more closely to God. I fought the fight of breast cancer and came out on the winning side. To God, be the glory for the things He has done.

Audrey Hicks

Age: 64
Florida
Five-Year Survivor/Thriver

ABOUT THE AUTHOR

Audrey Hicks is the mother of one fabulous son, named Michael, and the proud grandmother of four. She was born in Jacksonville, FL, and moved to Miami to attend Miami-Dade Junior College. Audrey had a 40-year career in the medical field in the administrative area. Upon retirement she was working in Oncology.

Audrey has been a member of International Masons & OES for more than 40 years. She belongs to New Shiloh Missionary Baptist Church, where she volunteers with several ministries. As well as being very active with her high school alumni, Audrey loves to travel, cook and entertain family and friends.

CHAPTER EIGHT

TRIALS—TRIBULATIONS—VICTORY!!

by Audrey Hicks

My journey started in April of 2009. One of my good friends gave a surprise birthday party for her daughter who was battling breast cancer. It was supposed to have been a get-together for her daughter to talk to the ladies about cancer. She did speak, and it really made me think because I have always had large breasts and every time I had a mammogram, the report was that I had fibrocystic breasts and it was nothing to worry about. She let us know what she was going through and what we should not do. Her main message was—Do your breast exams! Thank you, Gina, for taking the time to tell us of the importance of taking care of our bodies. Rest in peace!

In 2004, I started having an ultrasound along with the mammogram so that a clearer picture could be shown when I would have my annual done every year. Every year all of the reports always came back the same. In 2009, when I had my yearly exam, the regular tech was not there, so when I went in and there was no ultrasound done I thought that it was unusual, because the tech said that I did not need it.

When the regular tech returned, she noticed that I had already been there but that there was no ultrasound report. She, in turn, called me and asked me why it was not done, and I told her what was told to me. She told me that it was ordered and that it needed to be done. I went back in and had it done. Well, same thing again—the report stated that everything was fine. I started feeling and noticing something in my left breast, but I wasn't too worried because of the previous reports. But then I felt that it was getting larger, so I told my primary physician and she said the same thing: it was nothing—it was just because I had large breasts, and nothing showed up on my tests.

I kept pestering her and complaining until she sent me to get another opinion from a doctor that we both felt comfortable with because we knew him. In October, 2009, I went to see the doctor and he stated to me that it was a fibrocystic cyst and for me to come back in April of the next year. If I still felt uncomfortable with it, he said he would then remove it. I trusted him and had all of the confidence in the world with this doctor because I had seen him go through medical school, residency and internship, until he opened his own surgical practice. I had worked with him at several major hospitals and knew his work here in Miami. Mind you, during all of these doctor visits my family, especially my son, had no idea as to what was going on. The only person who knew and went to each and every visit with me was my godmother, Mrs. Dora McGregor. All the while, during this time I was planning and preparing for my family's first reunion here in Miami in July, 2010. So you can see that I had a lot on my mind.

Early in January, 2010, I went to see one of my Masonic sisters to get some paperwork done, and I began to tell her what I had been going through. She told me not to wait, because she had just been diagnosed with breast cancer and that she had decided to have a double mastectomy within the next two weeks. She told me who she was going to see, and I told her that she had an excellent doctor because I knew of his work and I had worked with him previously. I immediately went to my primary doctor and told her what had just happened with my friend and that I wanted a third opinion and she suggested that I go see the same doctor, Dr. Daniel Weingrad.

She called while I was in the office and made the appointment for me. He wanted me to go to the breast center and have a mammogram done, even though I had films, so that he could compare them. I went to the center and took my films, when the tech came to get me she informed me that the films I had had someone else's name on them. I got a little happy thinking maybe there was nothing wrong, but my inner mind said have the films redone to be accurate. So I told her to throw the films away and let us start from scratch.

After the visit of having the mammogram done, I went back to the hospital where I had the previous films done and spoke to the supervisor to let them know what had happened and to make sure that they were very careful the next time so that that would not happen to someone else. (They called it "saving film" by reusing it. I called it risking my life.)

I went to see Dr. Weingrad the next day. When he walked in he kept looking at me as if to say I know you from somewhere, but where? So after a few minutes I jogged his memory and told him and then he remembered. After his examination, he told me that he surely felt something and he measured it at 8.5cm, which is huge. He said that he needed to make sure, so he wanted to do a biopsy, which he scheduled for the next week.

My godmother was still with me because you can't go to these offices by yourself. You do not hear what the doctors are saying and you need someone to hear for you so that they can tell you later what was said. Remember, I said earlier that I worked on an oncology floor when I retired? Well, since I paid attention to what was going on when I was working, I knew the symptoms. I knew within myself, but I did not want to accept it. Mind you, if I had listened to what the previous doctor had said to me and waited and came back in April as planned, I would not be writing this chapter as a survivor. I wanted to go back to that doctor and give him a piece of my mind just to let him know that he had better listen to his patients when that tell him something--because *look at me!* My primary told me to leave it alone and concentrate on what is going on with me and get well.

I went and had the biopsy and was to return the next week for the results. I felt that it was time I told my son what was going on. I told him that I needed him to go to the doctor with me because they had found something on my X-ray. I went back for the results and my goddaughter was in town for her daughter's christening, and she went too. She had told her husband that, depending on the outcome of my visit, she would have to make a decision on whether she would be going back to Atlanta or if she needed to be here with me. I got the results and Dr. Weingrad never said to me that I had cancer, he just said, "You know." And I said, "Yes." He gave me my alternatives, which were surgery or chemo, because it was at Stage 3 and I did not need to waste any time because we needed to get to work.

He suggested that I try the chemo. I told him that I wanted to go home and think about it, and my son and goddaughter had other ideas. They told me that I was not going home to think on anything, that I had to make a decision now. So I chose chemo. I knew I was going to be alright because I know that God had not brought me this far to leave me. Dr. Weingrad made an appointment for me to go to an oncologist, Dr. Enrique Davila. I left the office and went to my church because I felt that I needed some spiritual guidance and I knew that my pastor would be at the church. At the time, I was the Lead Servant (President for those who do not know that particular phrase for a position in a ministry) of our church Kitchen Ministry. I had two other individuals working with me at that time. I told my pastor what was going on and that I had just been diagnosed with breast cancer, and that I would be starting chemo soon. I told him that I would need a leave of absence from my position and who I would recommend to be in charge during my absence. I told him I would give it to him in writing on Sunday at church. We prayed, along with the associate pastor, and when I left I knew I was going to be alright. At this time (i.e., before the biopsy), only my pastor, godmother, associate pastor and deacon knew what was going on with me.

Once I was diagnosed, my son, being the inquisitive person that he is, went on the computer and read up on everything thing that he could about breast cancer. He went out and bought me a drink from the Caribbean islands called "soursop". I had never ever heard of it. He came in the house with a case. I was up to my ears in this drink. I drank until I could not drink anymore. I was very proud and appreciative that he was that concerned about me. All that we have is each other. He is my backbone, and I am his. He even questioned the doctor about some of the medicines and to make sure about the drink so that it did not interfere with my treatment. (Only because of what he read).

Well, I knew of a friend of my sister who lived in Atlanta, named Sarah Grant, who had had breast cancer, and I called her and told her what was going on. She was my confidant and guidance person throughout the entire process. We would talk for hours. She never got tired of my calling. No matter what time it was, she listened to my tears, laughter and my pain. She told me some things to expect but not too worry about it. I love her for this. I may have never told her—but if she is reading this, I want to say *thanks so much.* You were there when I needed you the most. You will forever be in my heart and my prayers. I love you.

Well soon I was to meet my shining armor—Dr. Enrique Davila. He knew that I was scared and he reassured me that he was going to take care of me and we were going to beat it. I had a "pet scan" (whole body scan) done on a Tuesday. He wanted to make sure that there was no cancer anywhere else in the body. I had a port put in on Friday, and chemo would start on Monday. The chemo nurse was named Tomi, and she was the best! To this day I still keep in touch with her, even though she moved out of state.

The doctor ordered Ativan, and I was to take it one hour before I arrived to the office for treatment in order for me to be relaxed when I would take the treatment. (But I never did, as I felt I did not need it.) So Tomi gave it to me every time before she started the chemo, and I would fall asleep.

I took chemo every other week from March 19, 2010, until August, 2010. The off weeks I took an injection. Every Monday when I received chemo, Dr. Davila would come through the back door to his office and I would see him because I always sat in the first chair and he would put a thumb up. I would respond with a thumbs-up and then point toward heaven to let him know that God was also in control.

During chemo my hair started coming out so I asked my son to bring his clippers so that he could cut all of the remaining hair off. He was reluctant because it was Mama, but I told him that I would rather him do it than a barber.

God was so good to me that I was not sick, not *one day* while I was taking chemo. You are supposed to rest after treatment; however, I would come home, rest for two hours, and then go shopping. I felt good, and I thank Him for it. I would finish treatment and my son would have to wake me up and tell me that it was time to go home because this was not my home. I got pleasure talking to the other patients trying to encourage them not to give up. I would always tell them to trust in God and everything would be alright.

As I write this I am crying because I know how good God has been to me. My "god sister" told me that God had been trying to get my attention, but I was ignoring Him, so He had to put me through this test in order for Him to prove to me how good and faithful He is. That is so true because He will not put any more on you than you can bear.

After three doses of chemo the tumor started shrinking. It went from 8.5cm to 5cm. I could do nothing but give God the praise.

Well, you know how you try to be discreet and try and keep your secret. I tried to do this with my grandchildren. I would go to their house on Sunday for dinner and I would always have a cap on my head. They knew something was wrong because I never wore anything on my head around them, so they started asking questions. So I finally had to tell them and, lo, to my surprise, they told me that they already knew that something was wrong. My youngest said when his Mom asked him did he understand what I said, he said yes, "She said that she has cancer and that she is going to be okay". My granddaughter and her high school student government club sponsored a team for the Relay for Life for the Cancer Society in my name, and to this day even though she has graduated they still invite me to come every year.

Remember I said that I was planning my family's first reunion? Well, it was held in July, 2010 (I am still taking chemo during this time), and no one had seen me in a while, so when I came in my house everyone was looking at me because I had on a wig and everyone knew that I did not wear them. When I finished the introductions of everyone, I told my family what was going on with me. One of my nieces said she knew something was wrong when I walked in the room, because she knew that look. Her son is now cancer-free after being diagnosed with thyroid cancer at the age of four. He is now graduating from high school this year.

My nieces were very upset because they said that they would have come to be with me (they only lived two hours away). I told them that I did not want to worry them because they were still grieving over their father's death (my brother), and I did not want them to feel sorry for me, nor put that type of stress on them. I told my family not too worry, nor feel sorry for me, because I was going to be fine. We went to church as a family on Sunday to my church, and, as I was making a presentation from my family to the church, the Spirit spoke to me and I asked my pastor if I could say a word, and he said yes. As I told my story to the church as to what was going on with me, and why they had not been seeing me, there was not a dry eye in the church. I challenged every woman who was there that, when they have their mammogram done and are not satisfied with the answer, to continue pursuing it until you *are* satisfied because you have to be satisfied with what is happening to you. This is your body.

Well, I finished chemo in August. I had a lumpectomy in September because the mass had shrunk enough for it to be removed without having to remove my breast.

During surgery another mass was found hiding behind the first one, and the surgeon felt that it was cancerous because of the way it looked, but he wanted to be sure. So he sent it out to pathology. The doctor told my son that he wanted to wait for the results and if it comes back like he thinks it will, he will want to remove it as soon as possible. He stated that, had I had signed for the mastectomy also, he would have removed the breast so I would not have had to go through another surgery. That was on

Friday. I went to the doctor on Tuesday and the results came back positive, and I had the mastectomy on Friday. I went home on Monday to my son's home and I had the best caregiver anyone could ever have.

When I arrived, my youngest grandson was waiting at the door telling me to come upstairs because he had my room ready. That child was five years old at that time, and he is still that loving and caring person today. He made sure that I had everything I needed the entire time I was at his home. When the nurse would come he would ask her all types of questions, making sure that she was not hurting me. I love him for that and I will never forget it.

Now I began radiation. The first time I met Dr. Martin Keisch he scared the living devil out of me to the point that I had to tell my surgeon that I was not going back to him. When I went back to the surgeon, he called the doctor and asked him what he did to me. After they talked, I saw Dr. Keisch and he apologized to me and I found him to be a very caring and understanding person to his patients. I started radiation in November and was told that I would finish in early January due to the holiday season. On December 23, 2010, after a treatment, Dr. Keisch came in and told me to go home and have a Merry Christmas and enjoy my life because I was finished with radiation. I have been enjoying my life to the fullest ever since!

I had a little scare because when I went to see Dr. Davila in January, 2011, I was informed that he would be moving but he did not know where. I asked him what was I to do because I did not want anyone else. I said that I would pay out of pocket if necessary, because he had saved my life. This is how God works.

When I went to Dr. Weingrad's office for my next visit he told me not to worry because Dr. Davila would be working out of the same office as his because the three doctors had formed a group. God is awesome!

I have been blessed to have three of the greatest doctors in the world, and I would not trade them in for anyone else. God giving them the knowledge to take care of me and countless others is a blessing. I love them dearly and they know it comes from the bottom of my heart. They saved my life and I am now going into my fifth year being *cancer free!* I thank them and all of my caregivers.

It has become my passion to make sure that anyone that I see with a cell phone in their breast that I go up to them and tell them to please remove the phone because I would not like for them to go through what I did. So far, everyone has been grateful for the advice. I am in the process of working with other cancer survivors in my church to start a support group. We are making a presentation to our pastor concerning this.

To all of the readers of this, my story is just a small part of the entirety of what survivorship is. We all go through our own trials and tribulations, but we get through so that we can encourage others. It took me a while to even be able to say the word cancer, but I am making it with the help of the Good Master above. I am now getting to a point where I can see the stories on television about it. It feels as though, until I was diagnosed, you did not see that much on television, but now it is every other commercial.

Keep getting your yearly exam and continue to do your own exams. I hope I have helped someone to understand what trials and tribulations can bring and the awesomeness of it. You must have, and keep, a positive attitude throughout life. If there is anything or anybody negative around you, get away from it! You do not need that in your life. Don't let anything, and I mean *anything,* stress you out!! I have a stronger belief and faith in God, and I know that without Him I can do nothing. Continue to trust in God. Have a good life. Love you all!

This is what VICTORY is all about—it is living a life to the fullest.

Blossom Jackson

Age: 72
Georgia
Nine-Year Survivor/Thriver

ABOUT THE AUTHOR

Blossom Jackson retired from the banking industry after 20 years of service. She is the proud mother of five beautiful children (three boys and two girls) and has two handsome sons-in-law, three beautiful daughters-in-law and 11 grandchildren.

Blossom came out of retirement to open two small personal care homes for the elderly. Her involvement with the homes keeps her extremely busy and energized. She is active in her Church, Global EmPOWERment Ministries, located in St. Mountain, GA.

Four years ago, Blossom, her family members and friends founded The Hope Family, LLC, which feeds and clothes homeless individuals in downtown Atlanta. Currently, there is an extensive network of volunteers who cook, feed and distribute care packages to 150 homeless people every Saturday.

CHAPTER NINE

GIVING THANKS—IN MORE THAN

A THOUSAND WAYS

by Blossom Jackson

I was born on the beautiful Island of Jamaica in the parish of Northern Manchester, in a little district named Ticky-Ticky. I was surrounded by beautiful forests and mountains overlooking the Black River, and I spent my evenings watching beautiful sunsets. I am the youngest of four siblings; two girls and two boys. I was the baby, yet, I always had a lot of spunk. It was God's blessing, that spunk— my love of life and my determination to live that brought me through one of the most difficult periods of life— *cancer!*

My closest experience with cancer was with my mother. I remember that time long ago clearly. I was 21 years old. She was diagnosed in 1963. My mother was a faithful woman of God. She loved the Lord and stayed in the Word always. The night of her passing she served Communion at her home with three ladies. She sent two home and one remained with her throughout the night. They sang hymns, including "Jesus Is My friend, My One and Only Friend." Before they finished that song, my mother went home to be with the Lord. I was devastated! My mother was diagnosed in 1963 and died in 1963. She was 48 years old, and I was now a motherless child. When the doctor diagnosed my cancer, this was my closest reference point.

In 1970, I migrated to New York in the U.S.A. I built a good life, bringing my children with me. I lived there for 29 years and relocated to Snellville in September, 1997, to be close to my children and grandchildren. Leaving the snow behind was an added benefit. I was blessed to have all five of my children move within close proximity. My children were having children, and I was blessed with these beautiful grandchildren.

One morning in December of 2006 I was coming out of the shower and the Holy Spirit said to me "cancer." I wasn't quite sure why. I'd had benign lumps in my breasts throughout life —nothing serious. Why now? I was due to go and have my monogram in January of 2007. I kept my appointment and received a call from the hospital with a follow-up letter for a second monogram. I went back in February, 2007, and was told that there was some abnormal "thing." I made an appointment for an ultrasound, after which I had an appointment for the next Monday, and the results came 10 days later.

I did not hear from the doctor, so I just figured everything was okay. My niece took me to the doctor that Monday. The doctor came in and greeted us. I greeted him with a smile. He said to me, "If you were my mom or sister, I would tell them to have a mastectomy." I was shocked. My niece Donna reacted to the news by saying, "Auntie, you knew you have breast cancer and did not tell it to us." It was news to me, too! The doctor's assistant had forgotten to call me. The doctor was surprised. He sent his assistant in to explain to me why I was not informed.

Her explanation was that she put the note in her pocket and had forgotten to call me. She said that I have to do surgery over soon. Everyone makes mistakes, but in that moment there was no room for empathy. It was 2007 and I...*had*...*cancer*. I knew when I left that office that this doctor was not going to do my surgery.

The next few hours were a whirlwind. I gave my youngest son, Glen, the news first. I was supposed to go to Jamaica the next day for a wedding. His words were, "You can't go!" I then called my niece Sharon for help. This was a race to build my plan of action. Sharon is a Registered Nurse.

I called my friend, since her daughter had been diagnosed with breast cancer, and she had a good surgeon whom I contacted. By the time I got home, my appointment was made for the day after I returned from my vacation. I got all my last-minute things finished and ready. My final call was to a sister in Christ. I left her a voicemail...I have breast cancer. She called me back and we spoke for one hour. She said, "Before you tell me anything, let us pray." By 7 p.m. my room was full with my children, their wives and husbands. My eldest son, the man who was a rock, sat crying by my side. "Why, my mother? This is not happening!" I kept very cool and collected because I knew God is on my side.

It was 2007 and medicine, healthcare and technology had come a long way since 1963. My daughter-in-law Danielle and friend Arleen were researching the type of cancer I was diagnosed with. It's a blessing to have people in your life who will take the reign when you're running in neutral. My focus was on God and prayer. That's my neutral. The research they found showed that the cancer had a 99-percent survival rate. My son called me very relieved and said, "Mommy, you can go to Jamaica tomorrow." I politely explained that I'd never planned to stay.

I left for Jamaica and on the second night I had a dream. Paula White and two other people came to where I was living in Colleyville. They were praying and singing. As soon as they left, Joyce Myers came with two people praying and singing. One of the men had a bag and started to take weeds out of it and started to throw it out. I asked what he was doing, and he said he was throwing out the enemies. I woke up, and in that moment knew I was cured! The Holy Spirit had alerted me about my cancer and here I was being told it would be okay.

I returned from my vacation and my daughter, Nicole, and niece, Sharon, had my appointments set up with the surgeon, plastic surgeon and the oncologist. My daughter and niece had all the questions for the doctor. They were very thorough. I sat there and listened. Finally the doctor asked if I had any questions. I said, "Yes. Are you a believer?" He was taken aback. "Do you mean am I a Christian?" he asked. And then he answered,

PAULA SMITH BROADNAX

"Yes, I am a Christian." My next question was, "Are you going to see me before the surgery?" He said, "Yes." That was it.

Reality started to sink in. Four days later, I was upstairs in my bedroom and began crying. While my heart told me I would be fine, my mind was a blur. This woman with spunk was going to have a bilateral mastectomy! My body! How would things change? Something was being taken from me. I decided to go downstairs and get some water and call my friend Naomi. She beat me to it. The phone rang and it was her. I said to her (reduced to a babe), "I'm crying." She responded; "It's okay. Jesus wept." That was such an encouraging thing to say.

As time went on, there were many confirmations from God. The Sunday following my call with Naomi, I had a new resident who moved into my Personal Care facility. Her granddaughter dropped off her medical records the Saturday before she moved in. As I was reviewing her medical records, I noticed she had breast cancer. She was 91 years old and had it for 21 years! What a confirmation!

That Sunday was an emotional day for me. My spirit prompted me to call my pastor and another friend, Beet. Before the day was done, they both called me. This was truly God. I've learned that when there is stirring in my spirit, it's been placed there for a purpose. We talked for a while and they encouraged me. My heavenly Father confirmed with the three praying people in my life. I said to myself, "What more do you want?" That Monday my niece took me to a plastic surgeon. He took my measurements. The cost for reconstruction would be significantly less than average. I went back home, called my surgeon and told him. He said to me… two thumbs up to the plastic surgeon. He is very good. I prayed and meditated about it to get my answer. The answer was no! Do not do the reconstruction. I chose to leave that body part behind and move on. I would be whole without it.

Through my journey I've always put God first. I still had two more weeks to wait for my surgery. My daughter's friend was diagnosed with breast cancer about one year before me. My daughter was taking her to a conference celebration in Hartwell, GA. My daughter called me and asked if I could attend since there had been a cancellation. However, I would need to have a friend to be with me; like that was so hard for me. I picked up the phone and called my friend Naomi. Without even checking with her job to see if she could get off work....the answer was yes! "Nothing can stop me," she said.

The four of us started out that Friday to Hartwell. Upon reaching our destination, we were greeted by the ladies that hosted the celebration every year. They pampered us for the weekend (along with the other ladies). The Saturday evening my friend Naomi and I were standing in the sunroom looking at the beautiful water outside. As she was patting my hair, I said to her in a soft voice, just like a little child, "I am going to lose my hair." She said to me in her sweet voice, "No, you are not going to have radiation, and you are not going to have chemo." I just held onto those words.

We returned home on Sunday to get ready for my surgery on Friday. Friday, my niece picked me up and took me to the hospital. The aid prepared me for my surgery. Then, my little room was filled with my family. My son-in-law prayed and left for work. Then my doctor kept his promise and came to see me before they took me in for surgery.

After the surgery they took me to my room. I thought I was going to surgery! I said to my niece, "When am I going to have the surgery?" Her response was, "Auntie, you already had your surgery!" I was then taken to my room, my family with me. After they left, I went to sleep and had a peaceful night waking up at six a.m.

That particular morning someone came to my door. Since I had my head down doing my meditation, the person left. Thank God for that peace. My doctor came in about 8 a.m. and told me he took out seven lymph nodes and did not find any cancer. What a joy that was to my ears!

If we only put trust in God, He is there to answer our prayers. I was discharged from the hospital the next day. My niece came and got me and took me home. I relaxed with no discomfort.

Two weeks later, I went for my checkup and my doctor told me that I did not have to take radiation or chemo therapy. His only recommendation was that I take an oral medication for five years. Thank God, I am nine years out as of this January.

I thank God every day for His divine intervention. During my journey with cancer, I never one day doubted that I was not a 100-percent cured, and I held on. I am thankful to my Heavenly Father, my doctor, and my family and friends, for standing with me and praying for me. Most of all, I pray and thank God every day for all He has done for me. If I had a thousand tongues, I would not be able to thank God for all that He has done and continues to do for me.

Lucretia Jackson

Age: 72
Georgia
13-Year Survivor/Thriver

ABOUT THE AUTHOR

Lucretia was born and raised in Detroit, MI. She is an artist who also loves music and stays active by practicing yoga, dancing and walking. Lucretia also enjoys reading and loves to travel. She retired from General Motors after 33 years of service and now enjoys working part-time and volunteering.

Lucretia currently resides in Stone Mountain, GA, near her two children and three grandchildren.

CHAPTER TEN

MOVING FORWARD...

by Lucretia Jackson

It happened one day in February, 2002.

I was doing my routine breast exam in the shower when I came across "It". The "It" being the dreaded lump! At first I was startled; then I went into a brief panic mode, which I guess is probably normal. I then remembered that I had just had my annual mammogram two months ago. It was normal; so I relaxed a little, even though I was still disturbed by what I found.

Fortunately, my physical exam with my doctor was only a couple of weeks away and I was anxious to tell him about my discovery. He ordered another mammogram, along with a needle biopsy and an ultrasound. Several days later I returned to the doctor's office for the results. As I sat there on the table in the examination room, I tried to remain calm even though all kinds of thoughts and emotions were running through my mind. I tried to ignore the feelings that were telling me that this wasn't gonna be good.

It seemed like forever before the doctor finally entered the room along with a nurse. His somber look was a clue as to what he was about to tell me. He simply said, "It's cancer!"

Looking back, it's hard to remember what my initial reaction was. I think I was in a daze. Things happened quickly after that. He explained to me what my next steps would be. At the same time I was trying to take it all in.

The nurse set up an appointment for me to attend an all-day information session at a breast cancer clinic. This was for those recently diagnosed with the disease. When I left the doctor's office, I got in my car and just sat there trying to digest what had just happened. After a long while of sitting in the parking lot, I finally pulled it together and decided to tell somebody about it because I didn't want to carry the weight of this burden alone.

I called a very close friend of mine to tell her the news. She was shocked, of course. I actually had to say it twice before she could believe it. Once I made that initial call I hung up and then drove myself to work. Yes, I actually went to work that day! I didn't want to be alone. I needed to be around people. Later that evening I called my two sons, who lived in Georgia, as well as a few friends and family members.

The next few weeks went by fairly normally. I attended the breast cancer clinic, which turned out to be very enlightening, informative and actually comforting. I was blessed to have my close friend there to support and encourage me that entire day. One thing that I know, based on my experience, is that a person should never have to go through something like this alone.

We met with the doctors and the great news was that the cancer was in the fairly early stages. Also, there was no cancer in my lymph nodes. So the surgery recommended was a lumpectomy to remove only the lump and not the entire breast. I was also informed that it would be an outpatient surgery. Well, that didn't sit too well with me. As if the doctors didn't feel it was important enough for a hospital stay!

When another friend (who had breast cancer a couple of years before) heard about this, she was appalled. She strongly urged me to see her doctor, which I did. When I had the surgery, I was in the hospital for two days. I would like to point out that breast cancer (which I sometimes refer to it as "B.C.") is closer to you than you think. On occasion, I had taken this same friend to her oncologist for her follow-up appointments after her surgery. Lo and behold—here I sat, two years later, as a patient in the office of that same doctor. I recall seeing a poster on the wall at the clinic that was very sobering.

It said:

> *"If you're White...If you're Black...If you're short...If you're tall...If you're thin...If you're not so thin...If you live in the city...If you live in the country...If you eat all your carrots...If you don't eat all your carrots...The simple fact is, having breasts makes you a candidate for breast cancer and a great number will be affected by the disease."*

As I said before, the benefits of support from friends and family during such a time as this are a blessing beyond measure. I spent the first few days of my recuperation at the home of the friend who was there with me from the very beginning.

After a period of time I began my treatments with chemotherapy. People who had been through it would tell me all kinds of things about chemo and what it would do; so I was prepared to experience all those things. But I actually got through it pretty well. Maybe the chemo doses I received were not as strong as others; but I did not have many of the side effects. However, I did lose my hair everywhere, and I do mean *everywhere!* When I had to use a public toilet I would wonder why (when I would bend over to urinate) it would go all over the place. Well, it was because there was no hair down there to keep it in control! I lost my eyebrows, my lashes, and, of course, the hair on my head. But because I always enjoyed wearing wigs before cancer, it was no problem wearing them during recovery.

I began radiation a few weeks following chemo treatments. This was for six weeks. Again, I seemed to get through those treatments as well as I did the chemo. One thing that I remember is how I felt blessed to be able to continue my daily activities the way I normally would. I tried to stay active. I love to go walking, and I love to dance and hang out with friends. I continued to do all these things. My friends would comment on the fact that I didn't act like I was recovering from anything. The very same day that I finished radiation, I got in my car and drove 13 hours to North Carolina!

In the spring of 2003 my cancer treatments were completed. I was now ready to get involved with donating some time to helping others with cancer in some way. I walked in many breast cancer walks; but I felt like it wasn't enough and I wanted to do more.

I contacted the American Cancer Society to set up an appointment to do volunteer work; but for some reason I never got started. Things just seemed to get in the way of my finding time to do it. By the end of summer, I had made the decision to move from Detroit to Atlanta after some convincing by my son. So on February 13, 2004, I loaded up my car and drove to my new home. This date is significant because it was on February 13, 2002, that I received the breast cancer diagnosis.

I fell easily into the flow of the new chapter in my life being near my children and grandchildren, making new friends, finding a church home, getting around and learning my new surroundings. I eventually began getting involved in various activities, which included doing breast cancer walks again. It was always a special moment during those events when all the survivors were recognized; it made me feel so proud.

Finally, when I participated in the American Cancer Society's Making Strides for Breast Cancer Walk, I made it a point to go over to one of volunteer tables to sign up. I was given the contact information to call and set up an appointment for the volunteer orientation at ACS Headquarters. I was determined that this time I was going to follow through. The orientation turned out to be very informative and I learned about all the different ways there are to volunteer within ACS. One area of volunteering that was highly praised was a place called the Atlanta Hope

Lodge. After hearing about it I felt a spark of interest and decided this would be a good fit for me.

Hope Lodge is a beautiful guest house that allows people with all forms of cancer to have a place to stay for *free* while they are undergoing treatment at various hospitals and treatment centers.   The moment I stepped in the door, I knew I had picked the right place. I looked forward to coming in on my volunteer days to do whatever needed to be done. Everything from checking guests in or out at the front desk, doing tours of the lodge, or cleaning up in the kitchen. I bonded well with the staff and the other volunteers and I enjoyed getting to know some of the guests who came from many different places, even other parts of the world. I would get especially attached to those who had spent many months at the lodge while in long-term treatment.   When you're working in this kind of environment and you get to see what some of these patients go through, it just makes you realize that whatever you're going through is not so bad after all.

Before I knew it, I had been volunteering at the lodge for quite a long while, and during that time I was called on to do a number of different tasks outside my normal duties that also included using my artistic skills from time to time. There are various activities that are provided for the guests and their caregivers to take part in, such as crafts, yoga, games, etc. I was pleasantly surprised when I was asked to teach an art class. I was very excited since it was my first time teaching one and I was looking forward to it.

When the class began, some of the attendees were a little apprehensive when they first picked up their brushes to paint, but little by little they got the hang of it and then they were all in. My biggest joy was seeing their spirits lifting and watching their inner child come through as they painted and created their masterpieces. The class received such rave reviews I was later asked to do another one.

Then there was the time or two when the yoga instructor didn't make it to class, a class I also attended. There were people who had showed up for class ready to go. So who ended up teaching the class? Yep, it was me.

A couple of times I had been asked to represent or speak on behalf of the lodge. The biggest request I received came from the assistant director who approached me about speaking to women at a Bishop T. D. Jakes women's conference at Phillips Arena. I would be telling the story of my breast cancer experience, to which my response was, "What! Are you kidding me? In front of all of those people? No way!" She persisted in asking, I persisted in saying no. I just could not see myself standing up there nervously stammering out my story. I mean I've comfortably spoken in front of a room full of people... but thousands of people?

Then I was told that there would be someone else who would be going to tell her story, also. That didn't make me feel a whole lot better either; but I figured I could lean on her for support if I needed to. So, eventually I ended up giving in and saying yes.

The morning of the event the other woman and I were led to the backstage area of the arena where we waited for our turn to go on. I kept my mind in the present moment, not allowing it to think about what lay ahead. There was a flurry of activity going on around me, so I focused on that.

Finally it was time to go on. Amazingly, I remained calm as we were led up the stairs and onto the stage, while a huge round of applause welcomed us. I had no idea what to expect, so I was quite surprised when some members of the National Football League were on hand and gave me an autographed football (which was pink, since it was Breast Cancer Awareness month). There was also a bag of other gifts.

I was then greeted by Bishop T.D. Jakes' wife, Serita, and his daughter, who then escorted me to a chair. When I sat down and looked around I saw the entire arena filled with women. I didn't see a vacant seat in the house. The Lord must have had my nerves on lockdown, because I wasn't even fazed by it! Shortly after, I was handed a microphone and I calmly began to speak. It turned out to be easier than I thought because I was telling my story, I owned it. I guess that was why the words seemed to just flow out of my mouth. In my closing I urged them, actually begged them, to do their own self-breast-exam each month in between getting a mammogram in order to stay on top of things and recognize if there were any changes. If that weren't enough I even did a taped interview in front of TV cameras after I left the stage.

As I was leaving the arena, people were stopping me along the way telling me how much they enjoyed my story and how encouraged they were by it. I was on such a high I felt like I had reached celebrity status. When it was all over and I was at home that evening, I kept asking myself—did I really speak to over a thousand women today? I felt so empowered and so good about myself for stepping out of my comfort zone to bring some awareness to women about how important it is to be proactive about their body.

A few months later I was one of eight women who were honored as Breast Cancer Survivors by the Decatur-DeKalb Chapter of the National Coalition of 100 Black Women.

When I accepted this opportunity to share this journey of mine, I was somewhat hesitant about it because I didn't think there was much to tell. As I really began opening up my mind, I found I had a lot more to say than I thought. I had a chance to step back and reflect over the thoughts, feelings and memories that have been tucked away for a long time. You can get so caught up in the day-to-day activities; but it's good to just stop and take a look back and see where you've come from. Believe me when I say...I've come a long way!

Maybe that's what God wanted me to see. He truly had a plan for me that began that day in February. I can see His and all over every step I have made in this walk and I'm thankful for everything He has shown me. As I move forward, I know He is using me to be a light in someone else's darkness. So that they, too, can THRIVE in ways they could never imagine.

To bring you up to date, after being a volunteer for five years I now work as a part-time weekend manager at the Hope Lodge, the place where I feel I'm making my life count.

Carmen Rancifer Jenkins

Age: 57

Georgia

Six-Year Survivor/Thriver

ABOUT THE AUTHOR

Carmen Rancifer Jenkins is the very proud mother of three young men, Jacob, Matthew and Stephen Amos. She is married to Eddie and they love to travel and watch sports together. Carmen just recently celebrated 35 years of service with AT&T. She is currently enrolled in Strayer University's Master of Public Administration program.

Carmen is a very active member of Our Lady of Lourdes Catholic Church, where she is a Lector, Eucharistic Minister and Eucharistic Minister trainer. She is a "Scandalholic" and loves to read works by James Patterson.

CHAPTER ELEVEN

GOD, I WANT TO BE A COFFEE BEAN

by Carmen Rancifer Jenkins

To all who may read my chapter, I just want to say that, if you are one who journals, you already know that writing about an incident helps the healing process. For those who don't, trust me, it does help. You may not be one who journals daily, but writing or simply talking to an interested audience helps you to process the incident, and there is always that chance something you may say or write will help someone who may be going through the same, or similar, thing.

My story began years before my diagnosis. The family joke was I went and got in line twice when God was giving out breasts, and all my cousins who are around my age skipped that line altogether. Needless to say, yes I am well-endowed. I had a gynecologist who told me in my thirties, because I was "large" he wanted me to get a baseline mammogram then, so that when it came time for me to have annual mammograms, they would have something to compare it to. So I did as was suggested back in the early Nineties.

Fast forward: November, 2000. I had just found the dream house for me and my sons and we were preparing to move after losing my husband of 14 years. I had a pain in my left breast that I mentioned about to my doctor when I went for my annual checkup. He ordered a mammogram and ultrasound even though I was not at the "age" yet. I initially tried to explain it away. You know how we, as women, do: "I was lifting something I shouldn't have," "I slept crazy, it will pass," "I've been drinking too much caffeine," and on and on. Well, when his office called to tell me the tests had been set up, my mother was visiting and answered the phone. No more delaying now. Her questions were simply: what are they talking about and how long has this been going on?

Needless to say, I kept the appointment and went for the tests. They did find a very small nodule that I was told was of no consequence, but they wanted me to go on "watch." That meant mammograms every six months. Again, I did as I had been instructed, each February and August (my birth month). And I kept that up for the next seven years. No changes, just, "We'll see you in six months."

In the spring of 2008, I was having a conversation with one of my co-workers who had recently had a cyst removed from her breast, and I told her I had been on watch since 2000. She said, Carmen, get that thing out of you. I told her, when I went back in August, I would check into that possibility, but it had not bothered me in all this time.

During that time, my job responsibilities changed as well as the reporting structure. One of my good friends and I started working for what I promise had to be two of the most inept people in management history. They were wonderful *people*, but had been placed in positions they were not equipped to handle. So for us, a lot of the daily responsibilities that should have fallen on their shoulders fell on me and my friend's, since we had been around awhile in the organization and knew what was required. S-T-R-E-S-S with a capital everything! Couple that with three children in middle school. I had remarried and had a wonderful husband who also considering retiring due to restructuring at his job. The snowball was getting bigger. . . .

August, 2008, I went for my mammogram, as usual, and followed up a couple of weeks later with the doctor that my internist had referred me to, since I had told him I was interested in getting the nodule removed. He came in after looking at the results and said simply, "Carmen, you have cancer." I think I already knew. I didn't feel any different, I just felt that I was about to take a journey on a path that I had not planned, but I never feared because I knew *"Whose"* I was. I had told my director I was going to the doctor that afternoon to get the mammogram results, and for some reason, she told me to call her as soon as I left the doctor. I asked the doctor, when would we do the surgery? He told me we would have to do some more tests and, based on those results and other consultations, we would then schedule the surgery.

I walked out of the office, speaking with his nurse to get some of the tests set up, but, pretty much, I was just functioning. I got in the car and once I got out of the parking deck, called my director. Bless her heart -- she had left instructions that I was to be put right through so I didn't have to talk a lot to anyone, just her. I told her, and she asked me where was I? I told her I was headed home; "Good", she said. "I'll talk to you later and thank you for letting me know." Little did I know that she was actually on a conference call with two of my former supervisors. They picked up on the difference in her voice when she re-joined the conference call. She cancelled the remainder of the call. To this day her mantra is, "I hate cancer."

My husband was waiting for me when I got home. I told him, but told him not to worry; everything was going to be fine. God's got me. He said, "I know He does." When my sons got home, I sat them down and told them and told them this would not be an opportunity for them to act out at school or anywhere else. This was something I was going through for the glory of God. I really don't think they truly understood what I was saying, but they knew I was not going to tolerate any foolishness or drop in grades. So for the next few weeks, I went to appointments for tests, biopsy and tagging (they tag the breast, so they can find the area of concern easily at the time of surgery). I continued to work each day. That is how I dealt with everything, I needed to stay busy. I stayed positive with prayer.

My best friend Kathy and I talked daily, several times a day as a matter of fact. I called my college roommate, Adrell, to tell her. She said, "Let me ask you one thing," and I said sure. She said, "What is your prayer? Because that is the one I am going to pray with you." I thought for a moment and I said simply, that *God gives me the strength to accept His will in all of this.* Her response was, "Damn! That's a big girl's prayer!" We still laugh about that. And she did join me in that prayer.

Now, in all honesty, everything was not so smooth. My mother didn't accept this diagnosis well at all. I guess I can understand, your baby is sick and it's not a cold or a fever, it can't be fixed with a kiss, hug or pill. This could be life-ending. So, she and I had to have a long talk about faith and acceptance. I had to minister to her. She would call me every morning and truly bring me down. This is how the conversation would go.

"Hello."

"Hey!"

"How you feeling, Boo?"

"Fine, how are you?"

"Are you sure?"

"Yes."

"Nothing's hurting?"

"No."

"You sure?

"Yes."

"Everything else okay?"

"Yes."

"You sure? You're not keeping anything from me, are you?"

"No, there is nothing to tell. I have some more tests to get through, then the surgery."

"OK, how are the boys?"

"They're fine."

"You know, kids that age internalize, so watch to make sure they are not worrying."

"OK."

This went on every day for about a week.

Then one day she called, I got up from my desk and went into a conference room at work and asked her to please not call with the Schleprock (Flintstones) tone anymore. I needed positive calls, and while I understood she was worried, I truly wasn't. I told her I needed her to have faith like Mama (her Mom) did during her life. So, that day we prayed and the tone of the calls changed.

September, 2008. Surgery! We had to be there at 5:30 a.m. Kathy wasn't able to come, so she sent her husband to sit with my husband that day. The nurses at the hospital fell in love with both of them. They told me they knew I would have a quick and good recovery with both of them in my life. I was just hoping they didn't get put out of the hospital the way they were cutting up and joking with everyone.

The surgery was a success. I only needed a lumpectomy and my lymph nodes were cancer-free. I was totally elated, but too sleepy that afternoon to really do anything other than thank God for favor and sleep. I was on my way home by 4 p.m. that afternoon! I actually woke up enough to call work myself and let them know I was good (they said I was slurring -- LOL!). The boys were overjoyed to see me when they got home from school. A few friends called, but I slept most of that afternoon.

The next day, my two sisters-in-law flew in to check on all of us. One was a breast cancer survivor, so we spent a lot of time just talking about the experience. They cooked, entertained my visitors and kept my husband sane. When they left, my mom flew in and stayed a couple of weeks doing Grandmother-like things, like spoiling the boys.

I went for my follow-up surgical visit and the doctor was pleased with my healing. He said I would be seeing my radiologist and oncologist, and then I would just see him every three months, but know this: he and I had a five-year relationship that we were just beginning.

I only had to have radiation and finished just before Christmas. The staff and doctors are a special breed of people who work in that department. I did not meet anyone I didn't feel cared for me and my fellow patients' well-being. They were always so gracious and patient. Once again, I worked through all my radiation treatments. I had the last appointment of the day and went Monday through Friday. The hospital had special parking set up for us so we wouldn't have far to walk, and everyone just took care of us.

As I close my chapter, I want to leave you all with this story someone at work left on my desk one day and, to me, it put everything about breast cancer into perspective. It is titled, "I want to be a Coffee Bean".

A daughter complained to her father, who was a chef. She said that her life was hard and she didn't know how she was going to make it. He took her to the kitchen and placed three pots on the stove filled with water. After they came to a boil, he placed carrots in one, eggs in another and coffee beans in the last one. He let each pot continue to boil for a while. He then turned them off. He took the carrots out and placed them in a bowl, he then took the eggs out and placed them in a bowl, and he ladled the coffee into a cup. He asked her what she saw. She said carrots, eggs and coffee. He asked her to feel the carrots, of course they were soft and the leaves had wilted. She took the egg and broke and peeled it, realizing it was now a hard-boiled egg. But when she sipped the coffee, she smelled the rich aroma and the bold taste.

When she asked he father what did it mean. He explained that each item had faced the same adversity. The carrots went into the water hard and strong, but came out weak and soft. The eggs had been fragile, but came out with a hardened center. But the coffee beans had changed the water.

So which are you? When adversity knocks on your door, are you a carrot, an egg, or a coffee bean? Do you curl up and get soft and weak? Or is your heart hardened? Or do you face adversity and change the situation like a coffee bean? My prayer after that was, "Please God, help me to be a coffee bean."

Mary Jumonville

Age: 61
Louisiana
10-Year
Survivor/Thriver

ABOUT THE AUTHOR

Mary was born in the part of Louisiana call Acadiana, or "Cajun Country," that is, in Houma. The youngest of seven children, Mary began her career as jazz vocalist after finishing high school. She attended University of Southwestern Louisiana and then "took off for New Orleans" where she began to make a name for herself on the music scene.

She has played the New Orleans Jazz and Heritage Festival, and was a vocalist with many Crescent City jazz luminaries. Mary recorded with the likes of Ellis Marsalis and Allan Toussaint. She shares that some of the happiest times in her life were those spent with James Black, an influential New Orleans jazz drummer and composer whom she calls her soulmate and mentor. Black passed away in 1988.

Mary currently lives a half-hour outside of New Orleans in a town called Luling. These days, she continues to sing and make music in and around the "Big Easy" whenever she gets the opportunity.

CHAPTER TWELVE

KEEP SINGING, KEEP SWINGING

by Mary Jumonville

In the fall of 2005 my doctor found something in my breast. A blood test was done and that's how he found out I had cancer in my left breast. Following that, I had to have a biopsy at Our Lady of Lourdes Regional Hospital in Lafayette, Louisiana, which is where I was living after Hurricane Katrina blew me and so many others clear out of New Orleans.

Well, you get to the point after a cancer diagnosis, when the only thing you are thinking about is, "Now, am I going to die, or am I going to *live?*" When you don't have anything or anyone to help you through you *see* what you can survive. My family wasn't coming to see me much, except my daughter, Monique. I can remember thinking that I was glad of the diagnosis—well, *hell,* I thought, at least they can *cure* some forms of cancer. *At least it's not brain surgery I'm going to have to have!*

My cancer diagnosis was a miracle. I believe that God allowed the cancer so that He could see what I was made of, and so He could show *me*

143

what I could conquer. For me to survive cancer, even after the worst that Hurricane Katrina could deliver; after the divorce from my second husband (to whom I'd been married for nine years); and without even my family to come see me—that *had* to be a miracle! I feel that my family didn't come to see about me because they were just not strong enough. It was the same when my mother's had a stroke and a broken hip. In her last days none of them could handle it.

When I found out I had cancer I *had* to go to the Big Man. I quit smoking. I quit drinking. I quit pill-taking. He just took the taste of those things out of my mouth! The Lord just healed me! And if people don't believe *they* can't be healed; then they need to look at me!

It was cancer that got me down on my knees where I said, "I surrender everything to you." God did the healing for me, but He did it in such a vivid, meaningful way.

I was going to Abbeville, Louisiana to schedule my mastectomy and reconstruction. It's about 20 miles from Lafayette. My primary care doctor was a musician, and he wanted me to have the mastectomy with a doctor in Abbeville who, by the way, played the trumpet! I got good and lost, and found myself on *St. Theresa Street* in Abbeville. That was ironic because Theresa is my Confirmation name! I pulled over and looked up at a sign in front of a church where I was parked, and I said, "Well, I'll be durned." I saw the name: "Father Kenny Mayne, Pastor." Kenny Mayne was my *first* husband who received the call to ministry after we'd divorced. Now, why did I end up going to *Abbeville* and *not* Lafayette? Why Theresa Street? God is the Driver.

It was Kenny who came to the hospital after my surgery. I had mentioned to the hospital chaplains this strange "coincidence"—that my ex-husband, whom I hadn't seen in over two decades, was a Catholic priest living there. Kenny ended up coming for a pastoral visit, and the first thing he saw coming in the door of my hospital room was my big butt as I was bending over putting my clothes away in the drawers. I said, "Oh, excuse me!" And he laughed, "That's okay, I've seen it before." I told him about what I'd been going through, and after a while I began to cry, and he talked to me and soothed me. He anointed me with oil, which he pressed onto my forehead with his thumb as he read Scripture. When I said I had no one to coming to visit me, he said softly, "God is with you, Mary. And I am, too."

It was a *very painful*—and long recovery. I can remember that I went for more than a month without a breast, or any sort of reconstruction. For me, I think it was delayed for the consideration of my mental and emotional state because I was diagnosed as being bipolar. I *was* really worried that some of the medicines they were giving me wouldn't interact well with what I was already taking. They thought it was best for me to wait for reconstruction. I was one of the first people on whom they did the "Flap" surgery, where they take tissue from elsewhere on your body to form your new breast. I was cut all underneath, by my stomach—the incisions were really big! And after surgery I remember them putting something on me like a heating bag. I screamed and hollered at them to get that thing off of me!

My daughter, Monique, was only about eight or nine years old at the time. She *really* went through a lot. That's when we received this knock on the door, and it was the police serving divorce papers. So, she had to deal with cancer *and divorce*. And, since my husband wasn't in the picture, it seemed like she had the responsibility of taking care of me. I had to find some people in the complex we lived in to actually come by the apartment to pick her up and walk her to the bus-stop to go to school. Even so, she was very independent, and still is to this very day. I'm very proud of that. She would fix stuff for herself to eat (waffles and things). People from the Open Door Church brought us all kinds of good Cajun food. But often Monique would fend for herself, or bring me what I wanted to eat. She was always bringing me water with ice, because that's what I craved when I was recuperating.

When it comes to Monique, *she was there for me*. Though I wasn't extremely bed-ridden, it was still a strain on her. I think it somewhat affects her now. When children take care of their parents, usually it affects them later on in life. That child was my sole caregiver. She saw me in the bed a lot. I still haven't totally recuperated from that emotionally. It's hard to overcome. . . .

Spiritual sustenance is of the highest importance. But then, of course, you can't go without some good Cajun food. That's also what I recommend. And humor. It's part of the survival tactics that anyone would need. My whole family is like that. We make everything into a joke. So now I'm better—10 years in remission—and I'm looking for a tall, good-looking man with some money☺.

But, of course, I'm taking real good care of myself, and lately I've been involved with the local Council on Aging. They've been coming to pick me up so that I can go to aerobics class, and then they drop me off at home again. They keep you active. I'm very eager to get back my singing again. I have a friend named Angele Trosclaire who sings in the French Quarter, and she thinks she can get me some gigs. I'd love to perform again with the contemporary jazz band, Astral Project; or at Irvin Mayfield's new club in the Quarters. The other day I was telling jazz patriarch, Ellis Marsalis that I still have some of James Black's original material—his handwritten jazz compositions. Their music was the only music that was saved in the storm (Hurricane Katrina). There are tunes some people know in this bunch of music that survived, and there are tunes that people won't know. The papers look really strange—they look dark around the edges, like they're burnt! And you have to peel them apart—very strange.

The last time I went into the French Quarter to hear some music was to Snug Harbor, on Frenchmen Street, with the soul-blues singer, Carol Fran. Jason, the owner gave us the key to the apartment upstairs, and Carol performed. We had such a good time! And, now I'm staying with my friend Ava Somme, in her house in Luling. I feel so blessed. I feel we were put together for a reason.

God puts you through these trials…but they don't matter if you're in touch with Him. He will come to you. He is the Pilot. We can't thrive without Him. He's the Driver, and I knew that trusting Him was what I was supposed to do. We put a lot of "stuff" on ourselves, but I would suggest for anyone going through this experience to embrace the disease, and know that you can conquer it! Have peace inside yourself, and surrender everything to God.

CLOSING THOUGHTS….

As we finish the final edits of *We Survive to THRIVE! Volume 2*….I cannot help but wonder how many more volumes God has in store to be written. It is my utmost belief that the trials we face are not to punish us; but to make us stronger in our faith; to allow us to have a closer walk with our Savior and finally; to take the opportunity to share how we made it through with someone in a similar situation who might be having a difficult time.

These books are being written to leave a legacy with the world in hopes that our readers will be encouraged, inspired and motivated to keep moving through their experience. They are written to show others that there are blessings on the other side of through. They are written to inspire others to be bold and seek opportunities to share their journeys with others.

The phenomenal *Survivor/THRIVERS* that I continue to meet motivate and encourage me. Our encounters warm my heart and bring a smile to my face as we share. There is something special about them that allow us to have an almost instantaneous connection. Sometimes it's the greeting! Sometimes it is the beautiful smile on their face….a smile that comes from the inside out! And, sometimes it is the desire they have to give a hug.

There is something about these *THRIVERS* that reveals that they are truly grateful to be alive! This is why we share our stories…so that others can prayerfully see in us the beauty of a life lived for God's glory!

Paula

For continued encouragement, inspiration and resources to *THRIVE* in your life, join…

Our Legacy Creations community was created by Paula Smith Broadnax to inspire others to understand the value of leaving a godly legacy for the world and our families (historically and financially). Also, to….

- Motivate all to keep their *dreams* alive.
- Help others to understand that to achieve anything in life requires faith; belief in to oneself; having a vision; working hard; having dedication and determination.
- Inspire others not to give up or lose *hope*. Just when we are ready to quit, our breakthrough could be right there!! So, don't quit—just persist!!
- Assure others that the *possibilities* are endless if we decide to act versus react.

Visit: http://paulasmithbroadnax.com/legacy-creations/

→ Sign up to receive:
   * **Paula's Monthly "Legacy Creations" Newsletter** for Big Dreamers, Thrivers and Legacy Creators
   * **Paula's Pearls of Wisdom:** little insights to help us make the most out of life!

Plus check out…
   * **Paula's Pink Pearls Jewelry Collection**
   * Plus other beautiful **Breast Cancer Awareness** jewelry, tee shirts, pins, gifts and more
       Proudly show your support for breast cancer!

ABOUT THE AUTHOR

PAULA SMITH BROADNAX

Paula *Smith*
Broadnax.com

Author
Entrepreneur
Speaker

create, live and leave a godly legacy for the world!

About Paula...

Paula, a retired AT&T manager, held numerous managerial positions during her 30-year career in the telecommunications industry.

Upon retirement she decided to use the skills acquired during her AT&T career to become an entrepreneur and make her dream a reality after being diagnosed with breast cancer. Paula went on to become a successful innkeeper of a bed and breakfast inn (InnParadise) on St. Croix in the U. S. Virgin Islands.

After spending five years on St. Croix living her dream, Paula returned to Georgia desiring to be an active part of the lives of their thirteen grandchildren (who all live nearby). She worked for two years for the Department of Commerce as an Administrative Specialist during the 2010 Census.

As she continued with her entrepreneurial spirit, Paula wrote her first book, *Dreams, Hopes and Possibilities...a Breast Cancer Survivor's Story of a Dream Come True*. Compelling and powerful, the book details her journey from diagnosis to living her dream. Paula also started her business known as Legacy Creations to inspire others to understand the value of leaving a godly legacy for the world and our families strategically and financially.

Paula's life's goal is to...

• Motivate all to keep their *dreams* alive. And, to understand that to achieve anything in life requires faith; belief in yourself; a vision; hard work; determination, and dedication..
• Inspire others not to give up or lose *hope*. Just when we are ready to quit, our breakthrough could be right there!! So, don't quit--just persist!!
• Assure others that the *possibilities* are endless if we decide to act versus react.

paulasmithbroadnax.com
paula@paulasmithbroadnax.com

Paula's Books include:

• *Sisters' on the Journey* –
Contributor
• *Dreams, Hopes and Possibilities*
a Breast Cancer Survivor's Story
of a Dream Come True.
• *We Survive to Thrive Vol . 1* –
Collection of Stories

New Release:
• *We Survive to Thrive Vol . 2* –
Collection of Stories (available 10/2015)

Survivor to Thriver!!

Paula's Pearls...
sharing tidbits of wisdom

Her weekly email encourages many with inspiring principles for spiritual and personal growth.

Paula's personal journey has prepared her heart to minister to those who survived breast cancer (and other tragedies of life) by assuring them that they too can go "from a survivor to a thriver"!!

She spends any free time supporting her causes of breast cancer awareness and adults with disabilities. She is a board member of People Making Progress, Inc. which is a non-profit supporting developmentally disabled adults. Paula has been a member of Greenforest Community Baptist Church for 28 years and is also actively involved with the Cancer Support Ministry.

Paula and her husband of 19 years, Tommie, reside in Ellenwood, GA and have four grown children and 13 grandchildren.

paulasmithbroadnax.com

Survivors and Thrivers

Connect with us on

facebook.com/wesurvivetothrive
Twitter: @wesurvivetothrive

- Inspiration
- Author Interviews
- Breast Cancer Resources
- Breast Cancer Support Events, Cruises, Jewelry, T-Shirts and more

Visit

wesurvivetothrive.com

9 780692 518472